Living With Erectile Dysfunction Aint So Hard

Living With Erectile Dysfunction Aint So Hard

One Man's Story

Bruce Codrington

iUniverse, Inc.
New York   Bloomington

iUniverse books may be ordered through booksellers or by contacting:

iUniverse
1663 Liberty Drive
Bloomington, IN 47403
www.iuniverse.com
1-800-Authors (1-800-288-4677)

ISBN: 978-1-4401-8354-6 (sc)
ISBN: 978-1-4401-8355-3 (dj)
ISBN: 978-1-4401-8356-0 (ebook)

Printed in the United States of America

iUniverse rev. date: 11/02/09

Contents

Preface

So what would possess a man to open up, and write about a medical condition known as erectile dysfunction?

The answer is a man who has had to learn to overcome the heartache, embarrassment, depressed state of mind, lack of self esteem, feelings of being less than a man, thoughts of wanting to no longer live with this disability, and also a man that understands that there are so many men who are suffering from this condition and are not comfortable talking about it.

Just as there are so many men that feel as I have, there are also the partners of us men with ED who are suffering in silence.

Being open and honest regards to my personal testimonies does not make me an expert. However, in my heart I do trust that I feel the connection to many men that may be able to relate to my story.

I am not quite at the finish line in handling the frustrations and the answers to my questions of why me, but I am closer than I was when I learned that I was an ED sufferer.

So many medical conditions are making news in the 21st century.

We are all well aware of Breast Cancer events, the pink ribbons, the walks, the commercials on television.

We are also aware of the symptoms of depression sufferers.

When AIDS and HIV were the talk of the century, we embraced that in spite of the stigma attached to the disease.

Even several years ago, a famous blond television actress was a spokesperson for television commercials for bedwetting.

These conditions are just to name a few.

The media has done a commendable job bringing ED to prime time television commercials and magazine ads.

Print literature is visible in the waiting rooms at the doctor's offices, and at one time, several years ago even prominent spokespersons were doing television ads.

Even with all of this media attention promoting the three wonder pills that give relief to ED sufferers; one might think that the topic is open for normal discussion.

The truth of the matter is that it is not.

It is not normal for men to get together to discuss their inability to perform sexually with their partners.

It is not normal for men to let their guards down and admit that they are having problems getting an erection.

It is not normal for men to even talk about sexual activity unless it is in the context of having bragging rights to what a stud they are in bed.

It is not normal for men to admit that they have to take prescription drugs for a medical condition much less, for ED. Kind of makes a man feel less macho.

It is not normal for men to share openly with their partners their true feelings or fears about a medical condition. Although it is fine to share about finances, raising children, major purchases, where to vacation, career changes, and so on.

This condition makes for the lack of open dialogue that is needed so badly when talking about sexual intimacy.

It is no secret that most men hang their egos and sexual prowess on the head of their penis', which makes it that much harder to accept when they realize that their dick, is not working 100%.

In writing this book, it took much longer than I had anticipated. The reason was my pride and ego prevented me from being consistent to accomplish my goal of six months to completion.

Each time that I would have an ED moment, I would become angry all over again, and would lose my focus as to the actual intent of the book. I would then put my writing away for weeks at a time.

When I finally accepted that the book was not about Bruce Codrington, but about ED sufferers at large, I was able to press in and renew my passion about this subject.

One may not be suffering currently, but that is not to say that this condition will not strike at any given time or for that matter any age.

I have had many mentors, role models and associations with people from all lifestyles. Each has given me in their own ways much needed courage, strength and determination to speak my mind at all costs.

For that is the reason that I feel no shame or embarrassment by opening up my life to anyone. Each of us has a burden that we share, and in doing so, I find that we all are connected by many situations that are more common than we think.

Remember, out of someone's misery, there lay a testimony that may help another person.

Enjoy!

A Conversation Takes Place

It was around the spring of 2000, when a conversation such as this one took place.

You sorry ass, miserable, pathetic little shit!

Why is it that you always seem to manage to behave correctly, when it is just the two of us alone?

Huh?

Why is it that when I need for you to act properly when I take you out in the presence of a third party, you never do what you are supposed to do?

Huh?

Hey, you Dickhead, answer me when I talk to you before I slap you so hard that your ancestors will surely have felt it.

Moreover, don't you dare go cowering back into that pathetic state you love to go to either, because I am not falling for that bullshit any longer.

You have disappointed me one time too many, and I am sick and tired of always making excuses for why you cannot be at your best whenever I need or ask you to.

Damn man, I do so much for you.

I wash you.

I take you along when I go to the doctor for our annual physical.

I clothe you, keep you warm and protected as any man would for who has always been a part of him.

I mean from day one, we have been inseparable.

Oh well, guess when all is said and done, I have no choice but to stand by you since I am with you all of the time anyway.

Aint as though I can trade you in for a newer make, year or model. You and I are stuck until the grave invites us down under.

For that reason, I do want to do all that is within my power to help you.

I have done my best, but I think now the time has come for some intervention from a professional to try to figure out why you gots to act a fool more times than when you do not.

Perhaps before it becomes too late to salvage our relationship, the three of us can come up with a remedy for what ails you.

I mean there just has to be a cure or some form of therapy to keep your head up straight.

Shit, you try your best and too often, kicked in the teeth every time.

Such is life.

Okay, okay Bruce.

You can stop talking to your penis now, as it damn sure aint talking back.

Nevertheless, hey, this was just beginning to make me feel better. Hell, I could not have felt any worse having had to learn to live with erectile dysfunction now could I.

Other than talking to myself, who else can I blame for why my penis will not respond as it did back in the good old days of yester year?

I remember in the sixties when I was a teenager, I used to joke that if and when that time in my life would come to the point of not being able to "get it up", to just put me out of my misery like a Veterinarian would do to a lame horse.

A little extreme one might ask.

Think about it for a moment.

Life without sex.

What would be the point of living then?

Talk about pressure to not only have sex, but to enjoy it was even more of a challenge to be met, as I grew older.

How much worse could life get for a man without the ability to enjoy sex?

Gone are the days of being on autopilot when my penis would just take the natural course to full bodied attention whenever my eyes aroused my senses.

I had not a care in the world to worry about.

No excuses had to be made.

I mean shit, it was life as it was created to be lived, and enjoyed.

I recall those good times during Junior High School and throughout my tenure in Senior High, when I caught a sneak peek up one of my female classmate's dress.

Because pantyhose were not invented during the sixties, the girls had to wear garter belts to hold up their stockings. Thus no sheer material got in the way to block my view when eyeballing under a girl's desk while they were in a relaxed state, and more importantly not looking at me.

Often I was fortunate to have caught that oh so ever erotic view – when panty met with just good, old fashion, down to the bone, 100% natural thighs. My Lord, there was nothing like it that did it for me, and the best part was that it was free.

Just that brief moment of bliss would cause arousal in me.

When my little dickey became erect in school, I used to pray that the teacher would not call on me to stand to give an answer to a question. Therefore, I had to be real sneaky.

I used to sense that certain teachers were aware of boys getting a "woody" and would call on them just to teach them a lesson. Talk about being embarrassed.

One classmate in 6th grade must have been hung like a horse, because one time he got called on and everyone was shocked. It was a miracle that he was able to stand up. He was lucky not hitting his dick on the bottom of the desk.

Not that I could have imagined in my wildest dreams, that back in 6th grade, my teacher, Ms. Mallory, was deliberately sitting on the edge of her desk in front of the entire class with one leg hiked up just a tad higher than the other.

If it was done with honest intent for her comfort, or to get her jollies to tease us young boys, either way it was a turn on.

I read about what goes on in today's society with female teachers screwing their male students as young as 13 years of age, and have to wonder what must go through their minds. Better still, where were these teachers when I went to school?

Our Creator Does His Thing

Expecting that our Creator could, and would take away such an intimate, and up close and personal part of a man's anatomy made absolutely no sense to me.

Our Creator no doubt worked so hard to put our bodies together with the utmost precision to bring us joys and pleasures. It would seem a shame to have wasted all of the effort and time to just make my dick lie down and die alongside the highway of lust by the time that I had reached 50 years old.

There was a standup comic back in the 70's that did the funniest routine on the Creator in his workshop creating man and woman.

The routine went something like this:

> While the Creator was creating man, he was taking each intricate part out of his inventory to put man together. When the Creator decided to put the sexual organs in place, he was taking the itty bitty nerve endings off of the shelf one at a time.
>
> Each time that the Creator thought that he had sufficient nerve endings in man's penis, he would go, "Hum, think I had better add just one more little ending to be certain." Well this scenario went on until he used up most of the nerve endings for man's penis, therefore he felt confident that there were enough to make it work according to plan. Not realizing that his inventory was low, it dawned on the Creator that he still had to create woman. Since there were so few nerves left over, when time came for creating the

female next, unfortunately she ended up with less than man. The result is how we know it today. Men are so much hornier than women are.

I am referring now to the same Creator of the universe that created me.

The same Creator who has had a hand in the success of my 36 years of marriage to my best friend and wife, Janice. I would not have made it to this point and time in my life if not for my faith in our Creator.

So certainly, it is not that I have little to no faith, nor do I not believe in a reason for some of us men cursed in this manner. I just do not understand it at all.

It is so ironic that the Creator gave women different breast sizes, and men different penis sizes. Not all of us were created equal.

Those attributes in each gender have so much importance placed upon them. So much so that many a female are getting breast augmentations at such an alarming rate.

Females will cross that line of going under the knife or having needles stuck in their body parts to alter their look.

Now I may be missing something here, but I have not heard of too many men flocking to plastic surgeons for bigger penises.

Men may try those enhancements for $29.95 that they read in a men's magazine or heard about on radio to add inches to their manhood. However, that is the extent of their urge to be more well endowed.

For men, size matters until you get older. Then what matters the most, regardless of your penis size, is that you can get an erection at all.

Oh how our priorities change to keep up with the times.

Where in the hell did erectile dysfunction come from anyway?

Who created it, God?

Who the hell asked for it, me?

Who decides who gets the privilege of wearing the badge of honor that says, "I suffer from ED, and hating it"?

I could give two hoots as to the statistics on this dysfunction of the male sex organ.

I care less as to the reasons for the cause, and the all so famous, "it can be all in the mind" theory.

None of this matters, and why should I really give a gnat's ass.

All I want to do is to be able to continue having the most beautiful, intimate and fulfilling relationship with my best friend, lover and wife until death do us apart.

Is that asking too much?

Nothing else is as important as when you have that deep down feeling in your being that reminds you of that which you are missing out on, and you can't do shit about it.

An old saying (and by the way, I will be using several of them throughout this book) goes like this, "You never miss your water 'til your well runs dry."

And So It Came Into My Life

"Ah shit. Don't do this to me now," I cried out under my breath.

Again, there was Bruce talking to my penis.

I rolled over to my side of the bed, pissed off and cussing to myself; a scene that I had become all too familiar with. My sweet, adoring, loving wife who always has a way of making things right for her family, especially the children and me, responded to my attitude with the same comforting words as always.

While her soft, delicate fingers were caressing my back, she began whispering her comforting words into my ear. I was too embarrassed to even turn and look at her.

"It's okay, don't be so hard on (no pun intended) yourself," Janice said. "I am not going anywhere, and there will be other times. We can just lay here and cuddle."

Without turning my head to look into her beautiful eyes, I just said to myself, "Lay here and cuddle? Lay here and cuddle?"

Was she serious or delirious?

Were her words of comfort supposed to make me feel more like a man?

Cuddling would have meant a substitution for making passionate love to each other, and although Janice meant well in her heart, somehow at the time it just was not doing it for me.

Sounded good in theory, but this is not a make believe reality show. This is the real deal, and real men just do not respond after failing in the lovemaking department with simply, "Okay dear. You are right. There will be other times and of course I would love to just lie next to you, snuggle up close until we both fall off to sleep."

I would have loved to feel those words in my heart at the time, but the truth was it would not have been sincere. I chose not to say anything at all.

Less I forget that I had only drawn a bubble bath for the two of us.

Lighted candles for us.

Poured the wine for us.

Placed our favorite jazz CD's in the player for us.

Put on something sexy for us.

Removed my week of facial stubbles for us.

Most of all I had waited all day thinking about this moment for us.

I had sent suggestive emails and left voice messages of the same during the day.

Now was I supposed to be okay with just a cuddle or two?

No, I think not.

Failure to perform sexually, or better still, not even getting to the beginning stages of being able to perform just deflates the male ego to the highest degree. Any male that says differently is not being truthful.

PERIOD!

When I think back to the comedian's routine, I would often wonder if what women lacked by the Creator running out of nerve endings for their sex organs, that they were over compensated with nerves for extra sensitivity regards to compassion.

It is no secret that women are more apt to be the calming force behind any good man in a relationship, so in a way I should not have expected anything less from my loving Janice.

Bless her little heart.

As Fridays had become to be our date night, we had always made the effort to make for a special evening that was free from the telephone, television, and thoughts of our hectic workweek.

The rule was we each got 20 minutes to talk about our workweek, and then we were done.

Besides, after many years of being married, we understood the need to keep romance alive and on the front burner so that we would grow stronger in our love and intimacy.

This understanding is sadly missing from many marriages.

Lack of being on top of the romance in your relationship can and does lead to infidelity, dishonesty and ultimately too often divorce.

A Janice and Bruce Friday night was like no other. We felt that our date nights have been truly instrumental in keeping our marriage alive for 36 years and counting.

Our normal Monday through Thursday routine consisted of going to work, coming home stressed, tired, and just having enough energy to say good evening to each other and then good night. We hardly ever spoke, much less sat down to the table to break bread as one.

I used to joke with people that Janice once suggested we turn our kitchen into a larger family room as seems the only times we used it was for Thanksgiving and Christmas. We ate either out a lot or not at all.

So on this night of divine, of all nights, it made me even angrier since this was our special night and I felt that I had every right to be pissed off and cheated. All the while, I tried my hardest not to show it.

My not trying to show my emotion never did work though. If earning an award for my acting skills were in order, I would never take home the prize.

A Call To Action

I remember the first time that I had spoken to my physician on the subject because ED had already become an issue within our relationship. However, the first few times that ED reared its ugly head, I did not know that it would become a permanent problem.

Beginning from the summer of 1998, I had been under immense pressure that would last for the next three years thereafter. This pressure stemmed from the following family issues.

One of my favorite aunts passed away suddenly in June of 1998, leaving behind Uncle Felix after 40 years of marriage.

My dad, who was Uncle Felix's younger brother, came down from New York to visit us in Atlanta that November to quote, "get away."

The stress of watching his brother begin to come unglued over the loss of his wife was taking its toll. They lived only 25 minutes from each other in New York, so he was with him damn near everyday.

Dad visited for four days, and then on the day that he was to fly home, that morning I discovered him lying on the floor of our guest room, the victim of a stroke.

Once he recovered well enough for Janice and me to fly him back home, I then had to step in and handle not only his finances, but also Uncle Felix's business.

Six months later on May 22 Dad passed away.

After he was placed in a semi-nursing home, I personally felt that he no longer had the will to live in a handicapped state.

My going up to New York to visit him once a month took a lot out of me emotionally.

I then had to make a decision to sell the house that my father and Uncle Felix grew up in, and move my uncle down to Atlanta. He began experiencing early stages of Dementia.

He had lived in that house for 75 of his 81 years, so having to convince him that he could no longer live on his own was yet another emotionally draining situation to have to deal with.

Can we say pressure situations?

I, being one hell of a naïve person when it came to certain things, had not taken into consideration the stress and frustration that not being able to perform sexually had been causing Janice.

All of those failed attempts at intimacy she was nursing my bruised male ego by saying all that mushy comforting shit.

Really what she was echoing to herself deep down inside was like, "Look, this shit is messed up! Here I am all ready, willing, and able and what was to be fireworks turns into a big dud."

So how did I go about bringing up the subject to Dr. Price, Jr?

It was not easy since I was embarrassed talking about my manhood, or lack thereof. Yet if any person I would have shared this with, he would be the one.

Oh yes, he would be the only one.

Now that I looked back, it was actually in 1995 that I remembered casually broaching the subject in a round about way with Dr. Price, Sr.

He had been our family doctor prior to his son graduating from medical school and joining him in the practice.

The rules were when I visited him, was to make certain that I had some Black jokes for him, and he would always have some redneck jokes for me. We even had each other's email address for that purpose.

In 1995 I began to first realize symptoms that my "driver" was not staying the course resulting in not having satisfying sex all of the time. At first, I had just dismissed those episodes of non-gratification as one-time occurrences.

Dr. Price, Sr was a funny, old time country doctor, and his humor was included in everything that he said to you during your visit. I was confident though, that if he had to sit your ass down, look you in the eye to tell you that you had six months left to live, then perhaps maybe he would have been serious and omitted the humor – maybe.

I sensed that he knew what I was trying to say, since I was beating around the bush, so he gave me one of his funny, yet profound answers. He said, "If it looks like a duck, walks like a duck, quacks like a duck........ then you know the rest of the story."

Shit, I was paying $10 co-pay for an office visit, for a medical professional to tell me some bullshit analogy about a freaking duck!

He could then not let me leave without asking, "Hey, remember when you were in High school and you could hang a wet towel on your hard on pecker, and it would not sag?"

I laughed because I could remember those days in the locker room, and now I was not laughing as those good old days were obviously now in the past.

Now five years had gone by, and now there I was sitting in the examining room waiting for his son to come in to talk to me about what brought me into the office the first time in 1995.

The sweat from my armpits was pouring down the side of my torso, and my lips were hanging so low that I was not surprised that I was not folding them in my arms.

The month was May, and the year was 2000.

I will never forget the year.

Everyone was running around all panic struck and paranoid over the millennium, Y2K, an election, and all that shit that people worried about because of the media frenzy.

Some people were storing food, water, ammunition, forms of energy and all types of crazy stuff.

Funny but at the same time, there were other people planning humongous New Year's Eve celebrations to bring in the millennium.

Go figure.

It was in my opinion, insanity at its best for our society.

The year 2000 had gotten off on a happy note without any abnormal things happening. The biggest worry was God forbid our computer systems would crash.

The year 2000 was my milestone year.

It had become my long awaited opportunity to turn fifty years old that January.

Janice and I took our first cruise also that February. For both of us it was a major step out in faith. For me, I was paranoid about being confined on a ship, looking out at nothing but water and seeing no land.

Janice's fear was just the water. Not having ever learned to swim justified her fear. Nevertheless, proud to say we went anyway and took the plunge.

However, those happy occasions quickly were dampened when March came around.

My older brother, Stephen, passed away suddenly. His passing had left an emotional scar on me. At the time of his death, we had allowed 11 months to pass without speaking to one another.

Of course just as in most families, the being pissed at each other was over something stupid 11 months earlier after Dad's funeral.

However, no matter how small and petty the disagreement was, I had a hard time dealing with the fact that I was usually the bigger person of the two, and that I should have made peace rather than waiting for him to take the first step.

That incident had not been the first time that we had gone a long time without speaking, so I had just taken for granted that just as in years gone by, our paths would cross eventually, and we would bury the hatchet and move on.

Anyway, all that to say is that I had been reeling in my depression over my brother's death, so I also had gone to Dr. Price, Jr to get something to make me feel better emotionally.

Although I was against taking any type of pills, I was at the point of no return. I did not care what pill that it was; I just needed something to make me stop feeling so guilty 24/7.

I was called from the waiting room, escorted through the door to the workstations. My weight and blood pressure were taken, and then I was led into examining room number three to wait for Dr. Price, Jr to come and take all of my cares away.

I was sitting on that God-awful examining table, the one where they roll down that noisy paper to cover the surface so you do not leave your cooty bugs to the next patient, and vice versa.

I picked up one of those pathetic Fishing/Hunting magazines and began scanning through it while I waited for the good doctor to come in. How boring to look at bait, tackle boxes and all sorts of paraphernalia when you have absolutely no interest in that type of activity.

I have a habit when I visit a doctor, and I am left in a room alone for what feels like hours. That habit is looking around at everything in the room, and reading the Doctor's diplomas hanging on the walls.

Even if I knew by heart what was printed on each displayed diploma, I always managed to find something new and interesting.

As I sat and stared at his degrees, I thought of how nice it would be if schools indicated which percentile the doctor placed in the graduating class.

Therefore, as I was doing my observation thing, I happened to look down at the noisy paper that my ass was sitting on.

Would you believe that of all the advertisements to read on the paper, it was for a pill for treating ED?

My reaction at first was, damn just my luck, just what I needed, one more thing to make me feel like shit.

Then just as quickly as I got pissed, it dawned on me that at least there was a solution to a problem that I, and other men were having in the lovemaking department.

I was trying to keep my composure but I had been an emotional basket case for the past two months so it was not easy hiding my feelings.

My estimated wait time that day, was no more than a patient 10 minutes.

Usually when I am doing something stupid while waiting, that is when the doctor both knocks and walks in at the same time.

So in walked "Dr. Feelgood in Da Morning", with his broad smile and pearly whites.

He came with an air about himself as if to say; "Hi, what the fuck is wrong with you? I got my career, making tons of money, kids are all in private school, I am only 41 years old, and I get to make people feel better all day long."

Now of course he is in no way, shape, or form that type of human being, but that was the perception that I had conjured up in my scrambled brain at that point.

Jesus Christ could have walked into the room that day, and I would not have felt any better by his presence.

Dr. Price, Jr closed the door behind him still grinning from ear to ear.

He proceeded to pull his favorite stool on wheels over from the wall to sit his ass on, and at the same time he asked, "So Bruce how are you doing?"

That was the only question that I had to hear before I became unglued.

It was the moment that I feared.

I lost it.

It was not enough that I had felt like a pressure cooker with the lid on with no escape valve for the bent up steam in the pot, but the fact that I had to answer that one question, was in my mind very embarrassing and humiliating.

However, I was already there, I had waited, he was there, so not much else to do but to let down my manly ego shield of armor, set my pride aside and cry out for much needed – HELP!

Lord knows that if ever I had needed a doctor, the time was then.

Dr. Price, Jr must have thought that I was a candidate for one of those white jackets that fastens down the back, and your arms secured inside so you have no use of them.

The look on his face was one that I had never seen before in the prior years. But then again, I had never reacted like that around him before.

I could not have helped my actions.

I cried aloud;

"Doc, I lost my brother that I had let 11 months go by without speaking.

I sold my uncle and father's family home.

I had to move my 81-year-old uncle in to live with Janice and me.

I have an 18-year-old son getting ready to go off to college.

The stock market is tanking and I am losing my nuts.

Then on top of all of this shit, I can't get an erection."

"Whoa, calm down there buddy," said Dr. Price, Jr. "Things can't be all that bad as you are making it out to be."

"But you don't understand. I don't know just how much more of all of this that I can take," I said still in between sobs, and the snot running down from my big nose settling all up in my mustache.

I must say, I did take his advice in between my crying spell.

After calming down and listening to him, I was able to look at things on a brighter note. In addition, he reinforced the fact that in spite of all of my circumstances, that there were medications to correct those issues that were wearing me down the most.

When he had gotten me settled down, I waited as he wanted to take another blood pressure reading before I left his office. He wanted to make certain before dismissing me through his exit door that my pressure was back to normal from the 180/110 reading from when I had first arrived.

Hell, what would have been the sense of getting some relief from all of my cares only to go ahead and stroke out, or better still go and drop dead from a heart attack.

I would encourage any person that does not have a personal relationship with their family physician to do so or find one that goes beyond the scope of just giving medical advice.

If you cannot share your inner most fears, life issues and concerns along with your medical issues, then you need to find another doctor.

I will share a personal experience of mine with Dr. Price, Jr.

I got sick and tired of sweating like a Georgia mule and stressing out at the beginning of each annual physical. I knew that skipping my appointment was not an option, but I was racking my brain trying to come up with a solution.

In 2006, it had dawned on me the reason that I used to go through all those anxieties prior to my exam.

Men, I know that you can relate to this problem. I also hope that you are not eating at this point in your reading.

We always begin my physical with the normal upper body stuff. This includes the shinning the light up my nostrils, ears, and then shoving that God-awful tongue depressor halfway down my throat while asking me to say, "Ah."

Then the good doctor begins to feel around under my chin and throat area to make certain there are no lumps to worry about.

Working his way downward, the next part of this wonderful experience is when he places that ice-cold stethoscope on my chest and back. While asking me to take deep breathes in and out, he moves around to about eight different parts of my torso.

Satisfied that my ass is breathing okay and more importantly that there are no abnormalities in the heartbeat, he presses on my belly to make sure I am not reacting to any pain.

I always enjoy the next part, which is the knee reflex test. I always got a thrill out of this. I used to think weird thoughts of what if I accidently kicked him in the nuts when he tapped on my knee with that little rubber head hammer.

By then, I would be highly anticipating the next two tests, prior to being escorted off to the hands of the technicians for blood work, chest x-ray and EKG.

So with two cups of sweat that had accumulated thus far, the part that I had dreaded the most was about to begin.

As I slowly stood up, I followed the instructions to drop my drawers.

The drop your drawers was a prelude to the doctor sitting on his stool to be eyeball to my balls so that he can grab hold of them suckers, roll them around in his hands to feel for lumps.

Next, he presses into the area just above each testicle and asks you to turn your head in the opposite direction of which testicle he was working on, and then cough. Simply if he was pressing above your right one, you turned to your left and vice versa.

The finale is when he next asks me to turn around and place my elbows on the examining table, spread my ass and of all things he says, "Relax!"

While prepping for this most intimate part of my relationship with the doctor, he is placing ice-cold K-Y lubricant on his forefinger so that he can shove it up my rectum to check the prostate gland.

Yuk!

After he probes for what seems like an hour rather than less than 30 seconds, I feel as though I may piss all over his floor from the pressure he places on my prostate gland.

Now once he removes his finger, he hands me a couple of tissues to wipe the excess lubricant from my ass. He then strips off his latex gloves and discards them in the trash, and begins to thoroughly wash his hands.

Of course, he finds it appropriate to make me feel at ease as I am wiping and dressing to engage in conversation about the family.

Sorry to make this so graphic, but for us that have to go through it, is it not the truth?

This time as we talked I felt that it would not hurt to ask Dr. Price, Jr a question pertaining to my physical exam.

I began by saying, "Can I ask you a medical question?"

He smiled and said, "Of course. What is it?"

I said, "Are you taught in medical school to do each step of a physical in a certain order?'

His reply was, "No. Why?"

"Could you then do the last two tests at the beginning instead of at the conclusion?" I asked.

"Of course I can. Is there a reason?" was his question back to me.

I then went on to explain that the reason that I always got so nervous and perspired so profusely during my exams was the much-hated anticipation of those last two tests.

He laughed and said in all of the years that he had been practicing, he had never had a man bring that to his attention.

So from that moment forward, we get the "drop the drawers" part of the exam out of the way first, then I can sit back and be more relaxed knowing that the hard part is done.

A good analogy of this situation is a person hating the crust on the bread of his favorite sandwich. The person knows that unless you cut off the crust, you have to eat your way through that to enjoy your sandwich.

Now if the crust is eaten first, then the remainder of the sandwich eating process can be more enjoyable.

Had I not had that open rapport with my doctor, I would have not had the nerve to bring this to his attention, thus continuing to hate my annual exams. Something so simple has now made my annual visits more relaxed.

Dr. Price, Jr knows my background all too well. I have not kept any information pertaining to my health from him. What would be the point anyway?

He knows all about my being a recovering drug addict and that my preference for pills is not high on my priority list. However, he has a way of convincing me that in certain instances medications were not optional, but mandatory. In other words he would not take no for an answer from me.

I had refused for years to take blood pressure medication. I had not considered it that important so even when he had prescribed a pill, I would not even fill the prescription.

I would then pray that if I had an office visit in between annual exams that when the nurse took my pressure, that the indicator would not jump off the dial.

I had come to realize that I was not worried about the fact that I would be once again addicted to a drug, although it was for my own good. My real fear was from listening to Uncle Sonny back when I was a 16-year-old High School student.

Uncle Sonny was so open, and he would speak his mind regardless of your age or your shoe size. He had always felt that his right to say whatever was on his mind was just that – his right.

He used to spar with the late Sugar Ray Robinson back in his early days growing up in Harlem so he had a build unlike any of my other uncles or even Dad.

He was always in shape and because he had worked in law enforcement. He knew that he always had to be ready to kick ass. He had worked most of his career in Brooklyn and Manhattan and those areas of New York had the toughest criminals during that time.

Uncle Sonny knew that it was either him or them, and he was not going to lose any battles on his watch. Moreover, it was a pride thing, so he stayed in shape 24/7.

I used to love listening to all of my uncles from time to time telling stories about all of the fun that they used to have hanging out in Harlem in their heyday. From what I used to hear, they partied their asses off, and enjoyed the old time jazz musicians that they had come to know personally from hanging in the clubs so often.

One thing that always stood out in my mind from listening to their escapades in their younger days was that they all held down jobs. Even though they still had lived with their parents prior to getting married and moving out, each of them were always respectful of their parent's homes, and contributed to the household whenever they were paid.

During one, summer day, back in 1966 I was over to Uncle Felix's house in Jamaica, New York, and Uncle Sonny was there. He used to make his visits at least three times a week since everyone was retired. They used to tell war stories and discuss current events while sitting in the front room.

We called the front room, "the porch" because it had nine windows, three doors and only had a half a wall separating it from the living room.

They always had to sit in the front porch. That way they could be nosey and keep an eye out on what was going down on the block.

Everyone was talked about at one time or another from that block, and heaven helped a young person seen walking down the block in the middle of the day. The first question that would be asked amongst my uncles would be, "Why aint his sorry ass working or in school?"

Because Dad was still working as a bus driver for the New York City Transit Authority, yet living out on Long Island, he would be at his brother Felix's house the majority of the time when he was in between his work schedules.

On this particular day, Dad was playing pinochle with some of his close friends, so he was not at the house. In a way, I was glad. The following conversation that took place would have been embarrassing for me in front of him.

Somehow, Uncle Sonny got on this topic of health, and he was sharing his medical issues with us.

Because of his diabetes, and heart condition, he was on disability as well as retirement, so he was not hurting financially. He no doubt had to take a multitude of pills daily.

Just as clear as day, I recall him looking at me with his serious look and said, "Bruce, take care of your blood pressure. Because son, those damn medications will mess up your sex life."

At first, I was shocked that he would say something so personal like that in front of me, but as I said before, that was dear old Uncle Sonny. In his mind, it was like shit we are all men here talking about men stuff, so what was the big deal.

For me, growing up in the 50's and 60's children were taught to be seen and not heard when adults were talking. So being a part of a conversation where before I had never heard even my father or any other adult relative talk about sex made me feel awkward.

Good Lord, I did not ask what he meant by "sex life" for fear that he might think I knew that he had one, or that I was too naïve to not be active and not have one at my age myself.

I respected his sharing honestly on a subject that was on my mind as a 16-year-old teenager. However, the thought of not having a sex life before I even began was scary.

But I had never forgotten his words even now that I am 59 years old because it had made me aware back then that the possibility was always there to get to a point in my life where I may no longer have a quality sex life.

Therefore, now that I was at the crossroad of my life once again, I had no choice but to follow the doctor's advice and just take a pill to help me with my depression and another to help my erectile dysfunction.

I had read and heard all about the new wonderful little pill that gave men the ability to get and maintain an erection. There had not yet been that many advertisements on the television with different celebrities being used as spokespersons, so I still was a tad leery about taking anything when it came to my manhood.

My fears grew even worse when it came to taking a pill for depression since I still did not think that mine was that bad whereby it constituted a pill a day just to allow me to function. I had to decide while I still was sitting with Dr. Price, Jr if I was going to treat his medical advice on these situations as I had with the blood pressure pills.

I hate choices as either you do something or you do not based on how you are feeling at the time that the choice is made.

One thing that I had known for sure, I would rather not go on for years down the road with constant disappointments regards to our intimacy than to live healthy and not have a satisfying sex life as Uncle Sonny alluded to.

What was a man to do?

This choice this time in my life was a no brainer.

When the doctor left the room to go and retrieve me some samples, my mind had been made up. I was convinced that I did not care about any side effects or any type of addiction when it came to trying the ED pill.

As far as the anti depression medication, I could do without it. Further, what if the anti depressant pill prevented my ED pill from working properly.

Oh Lord, what a thought.

My thinking was that maybe if my sex life improved, then I would not be as depressed over my other circumstances.

This way the ED pill would be like killing two stones with one bird, or however the saying goes. How easy to justify a decision when it may be to your advantage.

I could not wait until I had the opportunity to try my new pill samples.

I took my little plastic bag with two sample boxes each containing six 25-milligram tablets of the ED wonder pill, and I had my samples of the anti depressants.

I knew which one of the options that I would sample first. If I had to be crazy, let them lead me away to the funny farm at least with an erection!

Would I have rather been normal, whatever the hell that meant, than have the ability to enjoy sex?

I think not.

I would save being normal for another day for now.

My priority at the time was to get back to having a wonderful, intimate, relationship with Janice, and if I dropped dead trying, or went off the deep end in a depressed state of mind, I was willing to take those risks.

Coming To Terms With My Ed

"Damn" said Janice, "Is this shit for real?"

"Now that's what I'm talking 'bout!" I whispered to my loving and supportive spouse of 28 years at that time.

Hell, what did I know the first time that I devoured one of those little sample pills of the wonder drug of the 21st century?

All that I knew was that the pill could not have made my shit any worse, and I was willing to cast all my fears aside in order to resume some form of normalcy in our sex life.

I must say, that Janice's question was legit.

I could not believe the response within 40 minutes from the time that I had swallowed the pill.

Dr. Price, Jr was right on the money with this.

It actually worked.

Hallejuleah.

Science and medicine made a believer out of me this time. Too often, you hear the hype, and yet the results are never what they are made out to be. Thus, disappointment and loss of faith in humanity become the order of the day.

One thing that a man does not need at the time he is already feeling down, and especially for this particular condition, is to learn that the remedy does not respond for him.

When I swallowed that wonder pill for the first time back in May of 2000, I was nervous as hell.

During my earlier years when I was 17 years old, I was a heroin and cocaine addict. This addiction lasted until I was 21 years old. I used to shoot each drug intravenously and often both at the same time.

I had little to no fear whatsoever about overdosing and dying. Back then, fear and Bruce were the best of friends when it came to doing drugs, and I shot up damn near everyday for four years.

Now going to prison and doing more than a year, scared the shit out of me. Therefore, to avoid any heavy jail time, I walked softly and chose my crimes wisely in order to get over on a daily basis.

I share that story to illustrate just what happened when my turn came to have to take legalized medications. I hated having to take a pill that was required everyday out of fear of becoming addicted again to a substance.

Because I developed asthma at 23 years old, it was a no brainer to know that my butt needed to use the prescribed medications to avoid dying from an asthma attack. If anyone has ever experienced one, it has to be the worse feeling in the world gasping for your every breath until relief came.

Of course what African American, especially male, does not have to take some form of pill to control hypertension? When my turn came to have to suck one down everyday, it was depressing as hell, but knew that it was for my own good.

Now back to that evening when I first took the ED pill.

I remembered as clear as day, that on that certain Friday evening in May, I was sitting in our basement, nestled comfortably in our leather sectional, watching the big screen television.

It was normal for me to be where I was. Janice normally was upstairs in the bedroom watching her TV programs. We could never agree on what to watch together, so we accepted the fact that she loves those Home and Garden improvement shows. I on the other hand have a habit of just channel surfing. A man thing.

I had thought to myself, "Maybe, just maybe this evening we can try our hand at some romantic time. After all, it was a Friday night."

We had shied away from keeping to our Friday routine for several months since the results usually turned into disaster, frustration and then me moping around for days afterwards in a piss poor mood.

With a Friday evening turn out like what I just described, who wanted to go there anyway?

"What the hell," I thought to myself, "Why not give it a shot."

Nervously but with little thoughts as to any negative reactions, I took the big plunge and let it go down the old hatch. Then I waited. Moreover, I waited. The directions said that results might take place within 30 minutes of even up to an hour.

The clock was ticking, and like an asshole, I kept quiet as if the pill would work faster by me sitting still and not moving.

Can we say naïve or what!

The instructions also suggested that drinking alcohol, eating red meat and being overly tired might hinder the response time.

I followed the instructions to the tee. I loved to get my drink on, especially after a long hectic workweek, but I was not going to jeopardize the pill not doing its thing 100%.

It was not normal, but from time to time, Janice would come downstairs to see what I was doing or watching on TV. On this evening, I heard her coming down the stairs and I got paranoid.

"What if I had become aroused all of a sudden? Would she think that I was watching pornography and quickly stopped the DVD prior to her reaching the bottom of the basement stairs?" I thought quietly.

"Hey sweetheart what's up, nothing on TV upstairs?" I said

"Oh, just wanted to be here with you," she replied.

Damn. What a prime opportunity for us to just go with the flow as long as I could be assured that the flow was going to go somewhere other than frustration once again.

She asked if I had wanted some wine, to which I accepted graciously, even though I would not drink until I felt a reaction to the pill.

I was not sure as to why Janice felt the need to come downstairs to be with me this particular Friday night.

Maybe she knew that I had gone to Dr. Price, Jr because I was feeling like shit of late, and she knew that I was going to bring up the possibility of trying the ED pill. She also knows that I have a tendency to say one thing, and wimp out at the Doctor's office and keep my big mouth shut.

I knew how Jack from the story, "Jack and the Beanstalk" felt when homeboy just knew that he had himself some magic beans to plant. Jack knew his beans would make a stalk grow big and strong, yet was not aware to the degree of the power in those damn beans.

Well, by the time Janice came back down with the wine, I began to feel within my manhood a sensation that had not been felt in a long time. That feeling that used to be so natural and spontaneous was erupting down below and it felt so invigorating.

I am certain Janice knew I had bought home some samples, but I was still embarrassed to tell her that I had just taken one. It seemed too fake.

It felt like trying to pass off a beautiful gourmet meal that you said that you had cooked out of love. The truth was that you actually bought all the food prepared, and just placed it on your own plates.

Yes, you owned it because you bought it, but it was not natural.

However, this was not the time to take for granted that a miracle was about to unfold before our very eyes. No this was the time to rejoice if the pill would work for us.

Notice that I did not say, "me" but used the word "us." This situation for ED sufferers is not just about the "me" factor.

Now the most common response that I used to learn to deal with, was wondering for just how long my penis would stay at attention. Often it would get to the erection stage only to fail the endurance test, which was the most critical part of lovemaking.

I was so used to feeling as if I was ready to enjoy an entire evening of fun and romance, only to have my penis retreat back to his little world, thus leaving us disappointed.

Because a scenario that I had just described used to play out so often for us, I had no reason to believe that the wonder pill would be of any help. Yes, I was negative and had every right to feel the way that I did.

The worst part of man's failure to please his spouse or partner sexually, is accepting that there is little that you can do about it. Lord and the thought of just accepting it, smiling and shrugging it off, as not a big deal, is downright humiliating.

Therefore, while the negative thoughts are playing in my head, part of me is praying that I have finally found the answer to my problem.

The staying power was the most important to me, because men need to make certain that our partners do not look at us with that, "Is that all you gots to bring to the party?" facial expression.

Now that the feeling was beginning to flow, I could get used to that, and that was all fine and dandy. However, the true test was how long the sensation would last.

Mr. Paranoia here of course read the instructions further, which indicated that you would be good to go for at least four hours.

Damn, within 45 minutes I had the answer to my question of will it work. I was as we used to say back in the day, "Ready for Freddie!"

Now that my penis was harder than times in 29, the true test was yet to come.

While we were sipping our wine, I sipping ever so slowly, things was beginning to be reminiscent of the Bruce and Janice when we were in our 20's.

The TV was off by now, the Jazz was playing on the stereo, and we were just talking and sitting close.

One thing that I can say about Janice is that she has to be the most beautiful woman inside and out that, I have ever known.

As we talked, it became little to the imagination when Janice noticed my full Monty, standing at attention in my pants. She just looked at me and smiled. The truth was out. She just knew that I used the pill.

Her smile, my erection, the mood, were feelings that were so hard (ha, ha) to describe. So just let me say that it made me feel like a teenager all over again, minus the embarrassment of being asked to stand up in class to answer a question with a boner in front of all of my classmates.

Nah my friends, this evening was so much better.

This was a moment well worth waiting.

If for no other reason to be happy, the fact that I was provided some type of cure for what ailed me was enough for me. This did not matter as to the name of the ailment; call it what you want to, but a solution to my problem? Now that was a natural high for me.

The next issue we faced that evening, was shall we take care of our lovemaking right then and there on the leather sofa, or to go upstairs in the comfy of our bedroom with the Queen size, four poster bed.

Janice always took so much pride and attention to make our bedroom a place not only for peaceful rest, but to relax and the atmosphere and décor were always so sensual to me.

Should we leave to chance that this wonder pill would not last as long as the directions said? I mean the directions are for everyone, but everyone does not respond to pills the same. Would I be the one in a thousand that the four-hour window of time would not be applicable?

Being the skeptic that I was, I had feared that the instructions were written for everyone else in America but Bruce – as if I were very important to anyone.

Regardless, I had suggested to Janice that we stay right where we were, and enjoy the passionate moment while all parties were ready and more importantly able.

As I mentioned earlier, my beautiful, loving and patient wife always seemed to have her ideas of how to do things. Most often than not, her ideas always worked out so much better than mine.

So, for the past 36 years as of this writing, I have learned to listen and not only listen, but to actually take to task what she advised to do, and did it. No questions asked.

Some couples are comfortable outside the bedroom, while some are not. Sometimes the moment calls for a spontaneous combustion to take place, sometimes it does not. Sometime men think more with their third leg than their brains.

In this case, keeping in mind my past failures, Janice decided anyway that a special moment such as this deserved better than to turn this into a "quickie" on the sofa.

Men, please listen to your wives or partners when they speak.

I am not saying that they are always right in every situation. However, if we let our pride not dictate our emotions most of the time, then we can step back and truly analyze that what they are saying is often right on the money.

The evening turned out to be an incredible one for both of us.

For the first time in years, there was no pressure at all during our most intimate moment together. I can honestly say that I had felt like a new man.

Since you know that obviously the wonder pill spoke a miracle into the lives of Bruce and Janice that evening in May of 2000, then the next issue for me was why I had still felt as if I was less than a man.

Acceptance Aint So Easy

Now that the physical part of this love triangle between my wife, my penis and me was taken care of, what does a man do about the emotional aspects of this condition that we have been cursed with?

As men:

Do we accept it?

Do we resent the fact that this is what we have to look forward to as we age?

Do we sacrifice one prescription pill for another and say fuck the consequences?

Do we look elsewhere to seek validation of what manhood should be all about?

Do we take our frustrations out on our partners?

Do we shut down and say, "I don't want to talk about it?"

Do we continue to live in fear of maybe one day the pills will not work, or worse become banned?

After all you know, this is America, and history has proven that too often when there is a cure for something, for some political reason, it always is an issue of debate.

A result of these powers to be that have nothing better to do but create more issues to stay powerful, could banning these pills become a reality?

Okay Bruce, you are at least at the point where you had asked to be, so stop being so pessimistic.

Just enjoy the results and take each day and year at a time.

Some of the ways that I have learned to deal with the medical condition that we do not like to talk about came about by accident.

Perhaps some of the options may be a blessing to others that otherwise may not know how to deal with ED.

These different coping methods are usually preceded with a short story as to how these methods came into my being.

If anyone can relate to any of these scenarios, then I would suggest that they come out of the valley of doom, and back into the light of hope by giving ED back what it has taken from us.

Let us kick this in the butt, accept where we stand on this, and most of all understand that we are not alone and that our feelings are normal.

I was the type of person that once I found a solution to a problem, then Bruce would feel and feed the need to create a new problem to solve. I could not be content with just being satisfied to then sit back and enjoy the now, and calm of my life.

One minute I was on the verge of committing emotional suicide (could and will never have the nerve to take myself physically outta here) over my ED problem. Then the next minute I am elated that someone helped me with a cure.

Once that fire was extinguished, there I went going to look to build a new fire to try to put out. I was never certain if that way of thinking was the end all result of my years living with addictive behaviors or not.

I always remember telling people that once an addict has kicked his drug habit, then the learned behaviors to survive that lifestyle are still a part of you.

Often times those habits are good, and often times they can be to your detriment.

As an addict, I was so used to hustling and surviving each and everyday just to ultimately shoot up. Once that was accomplished, I knew I had to begin right away thinking about the next minute or the next day's activities to get over one more time.

That lifestyle was a constant merry-go-round that never seemed to end. My thinking had always been in a problematic solving mindset just to keep my defenses up and sharp at all times. It was called survival on the streets.

The likelihood of me ever getting that far gone ever again is slim to none. However, I needed to learn to work on myself more thoroughly if I wanted to keep my relationship with Janice out of the hands of the Divorce Courts of America.

That much I did know and understand.

Saying all of that to say, once I accepted that the wonder pill worked, and our sex life was so much more rewarding, there I went looking for another reason not to be grateful for what I had achieved.

Some people looked at reasons to be cheerful. I on the other hand looked for reasons to bitch, moan and have pity parties.

So what did we have here?

Within two months after being energized by the wonder pill, and feeling confident that my libido was back on track, I then began to feel sorry for my condition all over again.

Now wait a minute here Bruce.

Number one, you were blessed to get up off your sorry ass, and go talk to your family physician in spite of your embarrassment.

Number two, you had an understanding spouse who supported, and encouraged you to seek help. Further, that same spouse assured you that she was not gonna up and leaves you just because your penis was acting a fool.

Number three, the family doctor was nice enough to give you free samples that were enough to last you up to 60 days so you aint had to go in pocket for any prescriptions as of yet.

Number four, you take the pills in spite of your phobia about legal medications leading to addiction.

Number five, you ass – they worked for you.

Number six, you and Janice are enjoying the benefits of the new Bruce. As a result, your self-esteem is taking a turn back to feeling good about yourself in other areas of your life.

Are these not enough reasons to keep you calm and stress free for a while?

Apparently not, so let us explore the reasons why I needed to organize another pity party with Bruce as the guest of honor.

I can only give one sorry ass excuse for not being satisfied after fixing the one problem that was leading to so many other issues within me.

That excuse.

Good ole, fashioned SELF DOUBT.

The self-doubt excuse stems from feeling that good things that happen to Bruce will be taken away. Doubting that situations will stay fixed causes me to be always looking for alternate answers or a plan B if you will.

I do not minimize that which was once maximized on my issues concerning in relation to the Bruce scale, which was created all on my own. The scale placed issues that may have not been that serious to the top of the scale because I overreacted.

The easiest way to explain this is to say that at one time, the ED condition was of the utmost issues of concern on my list of priorities. That problem was maxed to the hilt over any other situation or feelings that I was going through at the time.

All of the "oh whoa is me" feelings that were at the core of all of my actions, thoughts and attitudes for months prior to May of 2000, were based around my ED.

When I had those tendencies, and I do have them more often than I care to, I would reflect back over my past transgressions, mistakes and fears.

Once there, I would go back into my own shell of a world, and shut out everything and everybody that was around me.

I had felt that I had a right to do that, and wanted that to be understood by those around me.

Wrong again!

Since ED is not just about me, I really did not have that right to go into my valley of doom and gloom whenever I felt like it. I thought that my moods and reactions would just go unnoticed by Janice.

Nothing was further from the truth.

What those actions told Janice, was that if the intimacy was not always on point every time that I wanted it to be, then I did not want to be near or dear to her once the disappointment set in.

I did not understand at first, and continued to beat myself up so bad emotionally, that I had not a clue that I was driving our relationship deeper and deeper into a no win situation.

As a man, I do not ask nor want for much in my life. All of my doings seem to revolve around the comfort and security of my family members.

Because I leave myself emotionally drained when I have these frequent pity parties, I still seemed to muster up that extra little something that allows me to provide for a family need.

At least I thought that I was providing what they needed, especially Janice.

The truth of the matter was, that as long as I was walking around as though I was dead but just did not have a chance to lie down, looking as though that I had lost my best friend, then I was not providing anything to or for anyone.

I thought that I had my mood look, or as Janice called it, "The Pokey-Face" down to an invisible expression. The look that had kept my little secret from the entire world.

My amazing wife reminds me constantly that when you live with someone for 36 years, you rather get to know him or her better than themselves. Words somewhat just go by the wayside in marriages that last over 20 years and facial expressions tend to take over where conversations left off.

So how did I make that conscious decision to give Janice her due in the "always right" category?

Easy.

I have accepted that Janice always being right did not necessarily mean that I was always wrong.

When those moments occurred, and I would be feeling like a complete failure as a man by not being able to perform in bed, as I would have liked to, I would talk about it more.

In the beginning of my discovery and acceptance stages back in 2000, I found the subject very difficult to talk about to Janice or for that matter anyone else.

Since talking to Janice made the most sense as she was the other person involved in the equation, I then began to open up my feelings with her.

Because Janice has the uncanny knack to analyze a situation while you are still not yet finished giving her all of the facts, she usually summarizes the answer before you are through.

I must admit that there are times when this becomes very annoying, but I could never argue her logic – and win.

Therefore, when we would have our ED fireside chats, Janice would listen, and then have a question or answer for me immediately after I said my piece.

A simple conversation like this would be taking place.

"Janice, why does this have to happen to couples that love one another as we do, and also why does ED affect us men who are not looking outside of their marriages for sexual satisfaction?" I would ask.

My favorite analogy question to Janice that used to really piss me the hell off was, "Why does ED not happen to child molesters, prisoners, rapists, or gay men?"

Janice would respond, "First of all, our bodies act in funny ways. At least you have a pill that you can take to overcome your situation, women do not."

Secondly, she would answer, "And how do you know that ED does not affect those segments of the population?"

I had never thought up until then that women even went through sexual dysfunction before the age of 50, and what do they do in their case. Whom do they talk to?

Better still, as husbands or partners do we listen or pick up their signals on our own?

Probably not.

I know that I was guilty.

I was too busy always taking my own needs and wants into consideration first. In addition, my thinking was one of how dare my wife not always want to be the object of my desires.

Therefore, upon thinking on her response, I then could not help but to engage in a conversation with her about times when she may not have been in the mood as often because she is getting older.

This feedback allowed me to realize, as we both are growing older together, that we are also changing together in our own ways.

Another thought that I could not understand was that there are so many wives out there just wishing that their husbands went after them more often. Therefore, any spouse or partner that had their man chasing after them for more sex should be thankful. This indicated that they were beautiful, sexy and desirable. So I thought.

I felt Janice had one of the rare husbands that did not need to have his wife wonder why I have not touched her in weeks, or even months as in some relationships behind closed doors.

Therefore, I was made aware that at times I was being a royal pain in the ass. When I was always making what Janice also called my "raise and lower the eyebrows move" which would be my mating call, she did not find it appealing.

She would look at me and say, "Do you honestly think that I find that a turn on?"

Hell, what did I know? I thought that it was cute.

When I would get the old, "I really am not in the mood" or "I am really tired," response, then my backup was the "Pitiful Pearl" look.

That look was in a sense me stooping to the level of damn near begging.

Yeah I know that was tacky, but a man's gotta do what a man's gotta do, even if the results may not turn out in his favor.

Now even with ED, I still would not want to concede and be the one not to initiate intimacy. I was so stubborn and acted as though I could just turn my dysfunction on and off, or place on the back burner for about an hour.

See how the difference between men and women are?

As a man, I would refuse to give in to my lack of being able to be ready and cast fate to the wind and try to go for it anyway.

A woman would prefer to not have to deal with the frustrations and disappointments of both parties and just be up front and say that she is not in the mood for lovemaking.

A simple, to the point approach, and saves so much time and negative energy.

The stubborn male pride and ego is a bitch.

As another Uncle of mine always says, "Jealousy and Ego are like gods that must be served at all times." For the same reason, those qualities in a man can lead to deterioration in your relationship that may be irreparable down the road apiece.

The part of me that constantly was trying to be the man that I once was, did not add to the healthy attributes of our good marriage. I knew it, and Janice knew it.

However, until I was ready to change my behavior, accept that I suffer from ED, and make the best of it, then making love would be nothing more than Bruce trying to prove his manhood.

That type of attitude of selfishness did not show much respect for my wife at all, and trust me she knew it.

When I finally threw in the towel, I came to a clear understanding that marriage and intimacy do have to exist in order to be happy. No question about that at all. I knew that by me playing games with our emotions that our situation would only get worse.

My revelation on this came to me on our 30th anniversary, just two years later from battling my reluctance to accept that I needed "Penis therapy."

October 30th, 2002, Janice and I had taken a five-night cruise to Grand Cayman Island and Ochos Rios, Jamaica. Before embarking on our anniversary excursion at sea, we had made up our minds that we were going to have the time of our lives.

Prior to that October 30, we had racked up a grand total of losing six close family members in just three short years. For that reason alone, we were ready for a much-deserved vacation away from it all.

The date marked my third cruise, and Janice's fifth. She had taken two prior to this. One was with my Mom, and the other was with her twin sister. What made my third cruise that much more special was the fact that this would be celebrating 30 years of love and marriage.

Our Silver 25th anniversary was marked by us renewing our vows in a real wedding. When we first married in 1972, I had to borrow my mom's wedding ring, I did not have two nickels to rub together, and it was on a Tuesday. I had to go to work the following day, and none of my co-workers honestly believed that I had taken the day off to get married.

We had lost every photo that was taken during the ceremony over the years, so our 25th was the ultimate thrill of my lifetime. Now five years later we were on our 30th.

Both of us had been going through an emotional roller coaster from 1998-2002, and more grieving than any couple should have had to bear. We felt that for our 30th, that we would treat ourselves well and take a nice cruise just to relax.

To say that I was not extra nervous during that time would be a lie. I had wanted so badly for each moment of intimacy to not be marred by me getting an attitude, thus doing the domino effect of Janice getting one also, thus ruining our 30th anniversary.

Therefore, with my mind made up prior to boarding the plane to Miami, that whatever happened, success or failure in the lovemaking department would not put a damper on our special occasion.

Now I said that was how I made my mind to think right?

In reality, I was so skeptical of myself that it was not even funny.

I always begin to pack at least a week prior to a vacation. Now my darling wife will begin the night before. Yet never once has she forgotten a thing and she always looks the most beautiful of any woman that graces any room.

While taking my inventory of my blood pressure and asthma medications, I was thinking about how many ED pills that I should pack without being too presumptuous.

It would be foolish of me to have expected that each night that we would be up to making love.

Just spending a day in the sun, eating like a pig for dinner, having several drinks before retiring to the cabin would be enough to make any person fall off to slumber as soon as their head hit the pillow.

Throw in the motion of the water lulling you to peace just added to the most enjoyable sleep I ever had.

The more that I thought about the pill count, rather than putting additional stress on me, I just packed one a day. If not used, no biggie, I would just bring back home.

If I had failed to mention just another of my several good fortunes since I first talked to Dr. Price, Jr in 2000, let me mention it now.

I was a doctor's answer to how patients should be with their doctor. For that reason, each staff member just loved me. Every Christmas Janice and I would deliver a plant or flowers for the office staff.

We weren't trying to suck up to anyone, we just felt that they took such good care of our family members as well as us over the years, that it was just a kind thought.

Janice and I would always schedule our annual check-ups the same morning within 45 minutes apart. She even felt comfortable having him do her female exam with the legs up in the stirrup thing. Naturally, his nurse was present for that part.

I often wondered how Dr. Price, Jr felt looking at each married partner's genitals on the same day. In addition, his knowing the problems that I was having with my penis, must have made him imagine us being intimate.

I guess as a professional it was no big deal to him. However, this was just another one of Bruce's weird thoughts.

Dr. Price, Jr had a personal nurse, Sarah, who had to be the sweetest, kindest, comical yet most serious staff member that he had. She was always there for our annual physicals, and office visits.

She always had some funny story to tell you in that Southern drawl of hers to make you feel relaxed before Dr. Price, Jr would come in to examine you.

Her daughter worked there as well, and again, the feeling there was one of being part of a family.

She knew that our wonderful health care system did not allow the ED medications to be part of your prescription benefit. With this knowledge, and since they both knew my problem, I would be allowed free samples during an office visit.

Of course, I was eternally grateful for what I would be offered. The problem was because I was in good health otherwise; I only went to visit once or twice in between my annual physicals.

From that time forward, I would simply call Sarah; leave a message on her phone to ask if she could leave me some samples at the front desk whenever I was running low. At first, I had felt funny since I knew other men probably needed these samples also. However, those feelings soon became a "screw them" mentality. No other person than me was more important in my eyes.

In general, most doctors' offices disperse samples to their patients. In Dr. Price, Jr's office, all samples were marked and placed in a bin under the front desk counter.

This way even if Janice was more available to stop by and pick up the bag of goodies then she would just stop in, and they would give to her.

This had to be the most beneficial aspect of this whole ordeal.

In order to maximize my tablets, I would cut them in half with a paring knife. I cannot tell you just how many times, that procedure had me on the floor looking for the other half. It would go flying across the room.

Once or twice, I even had to move my dresser from the wall because the other half would fall behind it.

I got nervous one evening while I was in the "closet" performing my tasks so Janice would not notice. I had dropped a half on the carpet, and thought that the dog had eaten it.

Yes, it would have been so much easier to have used a pill cutter, but again I was always doing shit the hard way.

I was so cheap that God forbid that I would have even invested in one of those pill cutters for about five bucks. This would have given me at least an even split down the middle.

I would even attempt to break in half with my thumbnails. That is when I had nails and had not bitten them off when I had gotten angry.

Well, that was like trying to shoot pool using a rope. The halves never came out even. I would then become pissed. However, do you think that would have been motivation enough for me to spring for the five dollars?

Hell to the no.

Another example of being penny wise and pound-foolish.

Now in most cases I would take uneven amounts obviously, because I did not split evenly. After awhile I ended up taking the whole damn thing. Therefore, I defeated the purpose of trying to save a lousy five bucks.

I was not looking at the glass as half full with this additional blessing of getting free samples. I still was bitching about the whole ordeal of taking a pill to have sex with my wife.

I had waited until around the first week of October to place my order with Sarah. The last voice message that I had left went something like this:

> "Hi Sarah, this is Bruce. Janice and I are going on a five-night cruise for our 30th anniversary. Well, ah, could you please leave me some samples at the desk? Thanks."

Everyone at some point and time has access to my four-inch thick folder, including the billing department. I used to be embarrassed when I first noticed that on the front of my folder were listed all my medications. I mean even the samples that I received over the years.

I asked Dr. Price, Jr once if it was necessary to put all my meds on the front of the folder, as I did not want the entire female staff to know that I suffer from ED. He just laughed that hearty laugh and once again reassured me that as medical professionals, they hardly are concerned about knowing that I have trouble getting an erection.

A funny thing happened when I stopped in to pick up my goods.

I had noticed that the little plastic bag was slightly larger than previous times. What was also nice was that the bags Sarah used were not transparent so one did not have to know what you are carrying out in front of a waiting room full of other patients.

Sarah must have read between the lines when she heard my message and left three packs of 25 mg samples. She would normally just leave one or sometimes even two.

That was the beginning of Bruce not making this entire disorder a not so dismal doomsday situation. I even got Janice involved in calling Sarah from time to time. Soon even stopping to do a pick up became the norm for Janice.

I cannot say just how much better that made me feel that she did that without realizing the effect that it would have on me emotionally, not to mention the physical effect also.

Learning to laugh more about this subject, made our relationship even stronger than ever.

Prior to making light of the issue, I would be so resistant to acceptance that I would be angry all of the time.

I must say that it did not make for a pleasant time for being romantic, as neither of us would know if the pill did not work, and men sometimes it *does not*, just how I would react.

Being on the defensive may work well while driving, on your job, and even when you are out shopping for a large ticket item such as a car.

However being on the defensive does not bode well in the bedroom.

That frame of mind takes away all of the intimacies in such a way that cannot be rekindled at that moment no matter how hard you try.

That truly sucks.

If I have said it once, let me say it time and time again.

I have the most understanding spouse in the world. She lives for her family and most of all she has always been there for me from the time that she was 16 years old.

I am so truly fortunate and do not mind sharing with the entire world just how much Janice means to me for close to thirty-seven years.

In order for this new approach to work, Janice would recognize when I was leaning towards an evening of romance. This did not take a rocket scientist mentality or to be hit over the head with a steel bat to read the signals, especially mine.

For us, a special evening is planning the mood from the morning right until the evening. I would email Janice at work, or leave her sexy voice messages on her cell to let her know just how much that I loved her, and looked forward to an evening of romance.

It helps when you are empty nesters, so no need to worry about if the teenagers are going out, what time, and then plan around their activities.

These little signals were different once I had accepted my ED. Now Janice was part of the preparation and sending out her signals as well.

Once we got home that evening, and she sensed the progression was leading up to an intimate evening, she would just boldly look at me and ask, "So did you take your little helper?"

Sometimes just to tease her, I would answer that I did not, and then just watch the reaction on her face. A facial expression as if to say, "Oh no you did not just say that your ass is going to attempt this feat with no help from the little wonder pill."

I would then give her yet another of my looks. This one she nicknamed my "Doe Doe Bird" look.

I would then laugh, and assured her that it was already kicking in so we can just relax, take our time, and let nature and medicine take its course - as long as it was within four hours.

Living With More Understanding

So by cruise time, we both felt comfortable in our dealing with handling our situation.

Now I think that I have this thing down to a science.

I have Janice laughing and being more involved in making sure I take my pill.

I am laughing more at myself, and making jokes in the place of being pissed off.

I am receiving samples on a regular so still is not costing me arm and leg.

Most importantly, our lovemaking is wonderful.

For this anniversary cruise, we also decided to just go with the flow and spend time doing whatever made us happy. Did not want to feel any resemblance of commitment to time to do anything.

This was a challenge for me, because on prior cruises I felt that I just had to be up at crack of dawn, make every event, eat everything in site, and feel tired and miserable by nighttime.

Janice has no problem sleeping often until 11 or 12 noon. She can relax so easily. I on the other hand always have to feel as though I am doing something.

The biggest step for me moving past the feeling of having to make love just because I took a pill so as not to waste it, took place on this cruise. In fact, often I was too tired from the day's activities to keep my eyes open.

What I learned from this voyage was that I was learning to be patient and more respectful. Not 100% at this point, but I was making a step in the right direction.

So now, we can move on to why Bruce is still throwing those damn pity poor Bruce parties over living with ED. In reality, I should have little to feel shitty about, but I still had some reservations as to my future with this thing around my neck.

One might feel as though I had nothing to be upset over. All of my bases are covered from a physical standpoint, but there is still something that felt funny.

Could this emotional part of having ED be labeled depression?

Oh dear God, let us hope not.

I am scared shitless of depression. Been there done that and got the tee shirt to prove it, so no I do not want to go there.

So where did these feelings stem from then?

I love using analogies from stories, movies, or books to illustrate my viewpoints.

In this case scenario, I will use the Tin Man from the Wizard of Oz.

By all accounts, he was a man.

True?

The fact was that he was made of tin, and someone had to oil him up quite often. This kept him from rusting into one position. Had he not had to carry the extra baggage weight around which made him move slower, he would appear to have been normal.

I felt that once I had the physical aspects of ED down to feeling comfortable that I could count on a satisfying sex life more than 85% of the time. Those results would, and should have done it for me.

Nevertheless, I had to learn next how to accept that my body was in need of an oiling up from time to time.

The extra baggage weights was the timing when I should swallow the pill.

Then I had to allow enough time to respond before the pill wore off became more of a challenge. In a sense, I did not want my body to rust into a position of a limp dick for the rest of my life if I ever am without the pill.

Boy these were depressing thoughts, yet was my reality.

Even with all of the support mechanisms that were in place, I should have been walking in tall cotton compared to perhaps many others that were not as fortunate. Yet, I still chose to feel like less than a man due to not being able to have natural erections all of the time, or at the very least when I wanted to.

Now what could be worse that not being able to get it up when the occasion was there? Not being able to get it up at all. Now that would be just cause to cash in my chips and call it a life.

I was thankful that I was not at the epidemic stage like some men that are not yet even 60 years old.

Here is the surest way to know that there is still hope for you.

The surest test that your plumbing are in working order, is when you wake up in the middle of the night or in the morning with an erection for no apparent reason.

Because I had experienced this, and still do, I felt that I was not ready to be hauled off to the glue factory.

For me, my biggest frustration was being aroused when I did not want nor need to be aroused. My challenge was to make my emotional state of mind become aligned with my penis and together the A + B would ALWAYS = C.

My equation was not the case. Once again, there were always alternate options.

Amazingly, the most subtle moments had led me to become aware of yet another ED sufferer without that person actually coming out and sharing his dilemma.

Back in March of 2004, Janice and I were at a church function for the Marriage Ministry. We took the task upon ourselves and felt that we had done a damn good job.

Of course, the main purpose for the ministry was not so much to have more Bible studies regarding relationships, but the goal was to promote more fellowship.

In that regard, we were able to let couples simply be themselves, while still providing Christian fun.

We had taken a survey prior to organizing the ministry, and the consensus was that Christian couples wanted just to enjoy fellowshipping with other Christian couples. The idea to have Bible studies, or meetings, was not want the couples had wanted.

Therefore, in March of 2003, we organized the first new tradition at the church, titled, "Black Marriage Month." Our beloved Pastor, a newlywed himself, gave his blessing to have the month of March dedicated to marriages.

After the first year, we did delete the word Black so as not to offend or exclude anyone non Black that may have wanted to participate. We also realized that interracial marriages were on the rise.

Janice and I had a bulletin board in the fellowship hall set aside, and then we asked couples to bring in photos of how they had looked when they got married. The board was not as full as we would have liked the first time, and we had felt that the reason was many couples were embarrassed.

We had to be reminded by some of the older parishioners, that a format of this nature was never introduced to this particular church.

In addition, some couples only had photos of them from in the club back in the good old days, before they had found the Lord of course. You know those photos where you are leaning on each other hugging, and what was typical on a table in the club.

A typical table "set up" consisted of your bottle of liquor, glasses, ice bucket, and a chaser. Let us not forget the cigarette being held in your hand too.

Since the purpose was not to judge anyone, this became so much fun and a big part of the celebration for the first two years. Many members got a kick out of trying to figure out who was who, so the second year was an improved turnout.

The funniest, and my favorite photo, was of our Associate Pastor and his lovely wife. He had the biggest Afro style haircut, had this scowl on his face that would kill, and had the gangsta lean going on.

His wife at the time of the photo was just the tiniest and innocent looking person in the world. By far, they had received the prize for the couple that changes the most during their 30-year marriage.

Oops!

Did not mean to get off on a tangent, but just wanted to set the stage for the story that I am about to share.

The month long Marriage celebration concluded with a Sunday Brunch held at one of our favorite local restaurants. The manager knew Janice and me, so we could always count on him to clear the date to host our group in the banquet room.

We had the room all nicely decorated and festive. We had another couple that had assisted us, for which we were so thankful. In total, there were 12 couples, which was the maximum that the room could hold. We would always sell enough tickets at least a month early.

A word game was decided on for a fun activity. The game would be played in between the meal, prayer, scripture reading of a marriage related Bible verse or two, and fellowshipping. The intent was to get to know each other in a light, fun filled environment.

As we had each person pick out a letter from an offering basket, we asked each person not to share with anyone, which letter that they had chosen – especially their spouse.

Why?

Each couple had to describe in their own words something about their spouse beginning with the letter that they had chosen.

We were blessed to have had our Pastor and his wife attend the Brunch.

Because there were several new couples to the congregation, it was beneficial to those newcomers to not only see, but hear that even the leadership was just another normal everyday couple just as we all were.

To say that the exercise was too funny for words would be an understatement.

By the time that we reached the fifth couple, many of us were in tears from laughing so hard. Each couple had been very open and honest, which in itself can be hysterical.

However, by the time Deacon Jones, who was the leader of the Choir ministry, had his turn to give an example about his spouse beginning with his letter, none of us were ready for the answer that he gave.

Brother Jones had picked the letter "I".

I had to admit that I was stumped trying to figure an example using that letter that would best describe Janice. Let me say that it was no problem at all for Deacon Jones.

He stared at the letter for a moment, then calmly looked into the eyes of his bride of 33 years and boldly proclaimed, "This letter stand for the intimacy that Blanche and I share."

Deacon Jones not only said it with pride, but he had a smile on his face that made everyone burst into laughter.

The few "ahs" and "aint that sweet," were shared amongst us all.

What that showed me on that afternoon in front of the Pastor, his wife, Associate Pastor, his wife, Elder Simpson, and his wife, was that the reality of marriage was that Deacon Jones and Blanche were normal.

Here was a couple that after 33 years of marriage was still enjoying the intimacy that they both felt from day one. Putting it bluntly, they were still having sex, and more than that, they were still enjoying it.

We all know that there is a difference of having sex, and enjoying sex.

Of course, the next person to use her letter to describe Deacon Jones was Blanche, and her letter was "R". Her answer was not meant to be funny, but it was.

Blanche was somewhat shy, unlike Deacon Jones, so it took her a tad longer to come up with how to use her letter to describe something about him. With head buried in both her hands, and shaking her head back and forth from left to right, everyone told her to take her time.

After several moments in thought, it finally hit her as to what to say.

She looked her hubby in the eyes and with a straight face, she says, "Well all I can say is that he is always ready."

Well we could have stopped the exercise at that moment.

Blanche had that kind of personality that did not warrant anyone to think that she was trying to be funny, but the laughter that followed her statement dictated otherwise.

It took her a moment to catch on as to what she actually said.

That coming right after he shared how they enjoy their intimacy had to be the best response from any of the other 11 couples.

How this falls into the issue of ED is that most everyone knew that Deacon Jones had surgery for Prostate cancer. It is no secret that after a man has his Prostate removed, that he stands a good chance to loose his ability to get an erection.

That quiet ED sufferer that I was sitting at the table with that day made me feel as though not all was lost.

Hell I still had my Prostate, and Lord knows I did not have any symptoms of problems with it each year that I went to Dr. Price, Jr for my annual exam. If the Jones' were still getting it on, then I ought not to be too worried or anxious over my situation.

The following week I attended the Men's meeting at the church. When the meeting was over around 9 o'clock that evening, Elder Simpson and I stood outside in the parking lot for a while just talking.

I always admired this person, as he was young, ambitious, and a true man of God. However, more important than all of that, he was so down to earth, and did not wear the Bible around his neck like so many hypocrites in the churches does.

He knew that I was a recovering drug addict so he shared his heart with me about he was not always a "saved Christian."

Like so many brothers in Christ, many have walked on the wrong side of the law, abused drugs, fathered out of wedlock children and lived a sinful life in other ways as well.

Elder Simpson and I had gotten on the conversation about the Brunch, and how pleased that he was to see the Marriage Ministry growing and so active. Prior to Janice and me joining the church, no such ministry was in place.

We had agreed that marriage was too important a component in our Christian walk to take for granted that couples that come to church are not having some type of problems in their relationships.

We both laughed about the answers that Deacon Jones and Sister Blanche gave during the exercise. I had laughed because I thought it to be cute that they were still chasing each other around the bedroom and being passionate about their sex life at 55 years old.

Elder Simpson on the other hand had laughed for another reason.

Since he had been a member of the church much longer than I had, and he knew the Jones more intimately, he knew that Deacon Jones had the hookup for obtaining those little pills.

After the Prostate surgery, he was able to use his condition from a medicinal standpoint and have his insurance help cover his prescriptions for his ED pills.

Most men, like me, are considered users for reasons that are not medical so our prescriptions are not covered which sucks. But hey, what can you do about it. That is our wonderful health care system at its best.

When Elder Simpson told me why he laughed during the Brunch exercise, it was because he looked over at Deacon Jones when Blanche made her statement. Deacon Jones was grinning like a fat rat in a cheese factory.

Elder Simpson told me that Deacon Jones talks about his ED pills as if a crack addict would talk about his drug.

Since at the time of the Brunch, I had not been aware that the brother was using an ED pill, yet Elder Simpson was which is why he found their answers to be so outrageously funny.

We both laughed that evening in the parking lot, and then felt it okay to open up and to share that I too was a part of that ED club.

Elder Simpson always managed to keep things in perspective, which was another reason why I loved and admired him.

Part of my seeking answers to why I had to be a victim of ED led me to people that I would never before entertain the thought of talking about this subject with. This brother encouraged me to reach out to others if I felt that it would make me feel better.

It was then that I found myself fascinated with the completely new world of living with ED.

I was determined that I would attempt to bring this issue to light in a format that was not intimidating, too serious, but most of all helpful to all those affected by the results of living with ED.

That old saying, "Smile and the whole world smiles with you, cry and you cry alone" is so true.

In learning to joke about ED only became an option when I began to learn to adjust my lifestyle into accepting that I aint alone. Just as cancer, victims are not alone. Bipolar victims are not alone. Mentally retarded victims are not alone. Blind victims are not alone.

Yes the simple fact remains. One learns to live with the hand that had been dealt. Whether you like it or not is not the issue.

As I had mentioned previously, I do not receive any medical co-payment benefits when Dr. Price, Jr gives me my ED prescription every July when I go for my annual. The first time that I went to have my prescription filled was back in 2004. I almost had a coronary when the pharmacist told me that each pill was $13.

"Damn," I said aloud.

It was a good thing that the pharmacist knew me well over the years. He did not take what I said out loud personally when I did all but cuss out loud about how the HMO's and pharmaceutical companies suck.

In fact, he practically agreed with me. Too often, we forget that pharmacist are just employees also, and have families to cover with health benefits. So they understand quite well and see it everyday how poor people cannot even fill a prescription because of the exorbitant costs.

I was so angry that I lived to 54 at that time, had never been in a hospital, or had any serious health problems. Yet as soon as I do get a medical condition, the medications are not covered.

Bad luck?

Hey, if living with ED is all that I can say that was wrong with me at that age, then it aint bad luck at all. If anything, I should have been grateful that it was not a fate worse than or equal to death.

Now that would be some rotten luck.

I remember that I had only asked him to fill the prescription for three pills until I could get more free samples. Even at that, I felt $39 for three pills was outrageous.

Therefore, with bag in hand with my three pills, I thanked him and left still angry.

To put things in my life into perspective and to be honest about myself, I must share that I am always out to find the easy way out of a situation.

My motto is that as long as it is legal, or at least no more than 90 days in jail (just joking), then I would be open to listening.

I am not one who ever enjoyed going to the doctor for anything. However if I have a cold, asthma bothering me, or anything that I would constitute as life threatening, then I was not too proud to pay an office visit to Dr. Price, Jr.

Before I would leave the office though, regardless of if I saw him or his Physicians Assistant, I always would ask for a couple of packets of free samples for my ED. Depending on the inventory that they had, I would never get less than two 6 packs.

I had still not reached the stage of having to take an entire 50 mg tablet, so I could always count on doubling my dosages. Worse case scenario after I would break tabs in half, that if I needed the other half, it was not a big deal.

So simple.

Because of this strategy, I can honestly say that the first seven years of using the pill, that I may only have filled three prescriptions out of pocket.

The male pride thing that had made me make certain that I filled my ED prescriptions at a pharmacy that did not have a female pharmacist still is part of my routine.

Perhaps one day the HMO's will view ED as a condition as medical and not just a "oh that is just too bad" situation.

It is my sincere belief that more men would and could have more enjoyable sex lives without having to take on a part time job to pay for their prescriptions.

Not only would this make for better marriages, it would also make for less men walking around with feelings of inadequacies because they can not get an erection.

When I was in my twenties, I was just coming into my own as a respectable, law-abiding citizen, as well as a husband and father. I still had my own twisted, yet what I thought to be real philosophies about this society that I live in.

I used to wonder why there always were shortages of most things that are needed for everyday living. I remember back in 1979 when we were still living on Long Island, that there was a milk shortage. A milk shortage! Of all things.

After that crisis was over, and then along came a gasoline shortage. People had to go to the gas stations on odd and even days of the week. Depending on what the last number on your car tag indicated your turn to go.

The stress and anger was so severe, that people actually lost their lives right there at the gas pumps. A patron that felt that someone might have cut into the line would often result in gunfire once his or her temper done got lost.

Our society has experienced shortages of teachers, Federal funding for programs, jobs, housing, and healthcare for our senior citizens, and the list is endless.

Let me just say that each circumstance of a shortage did not have to result in a crisis for the everyday citizen.

Sadly, one must honestly ask when has there ever been a shortage of the following:

Heroin or cocaine
Tobacco
Prostitution
Gambling
Crime
Murder rates
Suicides
Child molesters
Pornography
Illegal immigrants coming across the borders,
Money for sending people into out of space
Wars
Loss of thousands of lives in war overseas
Think about that for a moment.

We live in a society where there never appears to be any funds for the people that keep this country moving, in the event that they loose their jobs and heath benefits. We will not even talk about the travesty of the Katrina victim's situation.

The average everyday working stiff cannot even get a break on his health benefits because some person in authority says that ED docs not count as a valid medical condition.

Keep in mind, $13 for one pill in 2004. It is now higher.

Hell, that can amount to $50 to $60 a month depending on one's sexual appetite. In fact, at those prices, whether you may want to increase your sexual encounters to more than what it may be already, if money prevents that, then tough titty said the kitty.

Too bad, too sad.

Lack of money to fill a prescription can actually dictate your sex life.

I would bet my last two dollars to say that there are couples out there right now that cannot enjoy the quantity and quality of a happy sex life because of ED. The want and desire may not measure up to the financial aspect of it all.

What has this society come to?

Take two people who may love each other dearly. Both are faithful to their vows. Both are generally in good physical health, and desire to have sex as often as they would like.

Now imagine that their desires become prohibited because of lack of funds to fill a prescription that may be able to help the male suffering from ED.

It is my opinion and mine only, that a situation like that is just pitiful.

Of course, that is just my opinion as an ED sufferer.

I am also taking into consideration that on average, a couple in their mid-fifties or sixties no doubt have other prescriptions to fill that are in fact covered under a health plan. The fact that they are covered would indicate that these medications could not be sacrificed and no doubt important to sustain their good health.

I have a close friend name Shawn who is just like a brother to me.

We have been friends for over forty years, and counting. He had served not one, but two tours of duty in Vietnam. Back in high school, we drank more than our fair share of cheap wine, and smoked just as much pot to go along with it. That behavior was considered normal in the sixties.

Shawn had to be one of the funniest people that I have known in my lifetime. Shawn would also give you the shirt off his back if you needed it, no questions asked.

Sadly, the past 15 years have not been too good to Brother Shawn.

He has suffered from Multiple Sclerosis to the point of being damn near dependent on his wheelchair more than ever.

Then as if that were not enough to debilitate him, in 2005 he was diagnosed with Prostate cancer. He had elected surgery to remove to avoid all the chemo and radiation.

But can we talk about a man that never ever complains?

Shawn would get anyone's vote hand's down.

Labor day of 2005, I had gone up to New Jersey to spend the weekend with him.

Shawn had picked me up from the Philadelphia Airport for the 45 minute drive to his home just outside of Cherry Hill. We stayed at the house just long enough for him to show me around his garden, inside the house and his prize 1970 Volkswagen beetle.

After dropping off my suitcase, we both agreed that lunch was in order.

I was starving since we all know that flying in the 21st century nets you a cup of soda and an itty-bitty bag with 18 peanuts inside.

We had the usual man thing, cheeseburger with fries, and we sat and talked for awhile.

Shawn mentioned that he had to go to the PX store to look for a portable CD player. He was fortunate to be able to have access to the PX on the Air Force as a benefit for being retired from the military.

He had to use one of those motorized scooters while shopping. We had laughed about our school days when we could not even remember how we had made it home from partying to the wee hours of the morning.

Now there he was not being able to walk on his own without assistance.

I will never forget that when we were about to leave the store, Shawn had to use the men's room.

To accomplish this feat, he first had to leave the scooter, and then pick up his crutches or his "sticks" as he liked to call them.

The restrooms were just outside the PX but still in the mall area, and there were stairs to climb. On either side of the stairs were handicap ramps, which he had to use. Not realizing prior to this situation that I had not been conscious of the fact that I needed to slow my pace since he could not keep up with me.

All the time that Shawn was in the men's room, I found myself looking at one of the mall vendor's artwork on display. I was not buying shit, but I felt compelled to tell her how nice her artwork was even though it was not my taste.

I guess that she sensed that I was just killing time while I was waiting for Shawn. Then out of the clear blue, she surprised me by mentioning how much she admired watching "my friend" make it up the ramp on his "sticks."

She then shared with me how she never took her eyes off him the entire time that he was taking one step at a time.

I asked her if she had noticed every person that passed her booth, and her answer was no. I was moved when she said that she watched his expression as he struggled, and he always had a smile on his face.

I just took it for granted as he had been that way ever since I had known him.

Working at the mall, she said that she normally observes people bitching and being rude to one another, and they had no handicaps.

It made her heart rejoice to see someone who was handicapped smiling and just living life as it had been handed to him while making the best of it.

When Shawn emerged from the bathroom, she personally told him just what she had told me. She then asked him why he smiled so much.

Shawn smiled and replied in his ever so calm manner. He said, "Why not smile? I am alive, clean and sober, my brother is here from Atlanta just to visit me, and so I am very blessed."

No doubt, that the woman was blessed by what he said. I knew that I was.

After we had left the mall and the PX, I was given a grand tour.

He drove me around the military base where he had been stationed until his discharge in 1990. I was never in the military so the tour of the grounds did nothing at all for me. It was not exciting or interesting to me, but did not want to hurt his feelings, as he was so proud of that part of his life.

The part of the tour that did have me sitting up straight in the passenger seat, was when he drove me around the neighborhood where he had lived for two years prior to his sobriety.

He had pointed out a nasty, swamp looking, mosquito infested lake where he told me that he used to sit, drink, and fish damn near everyday after he had gotten off work at the base.

Most of the time he said that he would fall off to sleep and little fishing was ever accomplished.

He also said that a few times he was so drunk that he would wake up the next day after lying out there all night, and then get up and go right to work.

Just by his description of the setting during that time in his life, his words had me scratching. I could not imagine how a person could sleep out in the open amongst all of that infestation yet not be eaten alive.

Perhaps his training over in the Nam allowed him to deal with it. Plus when you are stoned out of your mind, you really do not think much about anything, especially your safety.

Once back at his house, we sat up half the night laughing, and reminiscing about the good old days during our High School years.

The following day we drove 90 minutes to Atlantic City and only spent one hour there. His having to use his motorized wheelchair did not mix well with the people that were there for one thing and one thing only – GAMBLING.

Although he tried to maneuver in the Casino so that I could at least say that I had lost my five bucks, I did not feel right that he was struggling. The crowd could have given two shits about his situation.

I made my five dollar donation, and then we got right back in the car and drove back to Cherry Hill. He let me drive this time. The time driving and talking meant more to us than where we actually went anyway. We went to dinner, talked and laughed some more.

In spite of my being there that weekend, did not prohibit Shawn from awaking early that Sunday, and attending his AA meeting at 10 o'clock. Since it was over by noon, we drove to Atlantic City afterward.

This brother had been clean and sober for over 15 years, and I am so proud of him. I attended the meeting with him, and was brought to tears by hearing the testimonials.

I have been clean since 1971.

I had not had to attend any form of addiction meetings during all of that time. However, for me this had so many memories of when I had to go to counseling during my prior failed attempts at recovery.

Man, what a reality check.

Present at Shawn's meeting were a former Police officer, a nurse who had lost her license for stealing medications from the hospital, an attorney, and just others from all lifestyles.

Shawn introduced me to his sponsor and the person in turn that Shawn sponsors.

As I sat there, wiping the tears from my eyes, I realized just how blessed that I was. I had to ask myself how I could feel so sorry for myself, and get attitudes with Janice just because I was having problems getting an erection.

Really now, I had just spent three days with someone that I have known for more than half of my life.

I had watched him take his handicap with a smile on his face, laughter in his heart, and a faith that could move mountains.

To this day I am confident that my visiting him did more for my spirit that his.

I share this story about Shawn to set the stage for my next example of how men can make their ED circumstances less stressful and add some humor to it.

Shawn had medical reasons to no doubt cause him not to be able to get it up with his lady friend Darlene.

Since he was a veteran, he had access to the Veterans Administration Hospital in Philadelphia so his visits and prescriptions were dirt-cheap. In fact he joked that he calculated that the gas to drive from Cherry Hill to Philly and back was more that the cost of his prescriptions.

Of course now that I shared what a wonderful person Shawn is, I can now say that he is not 100% cured of being trifling if the occasion called for it.

I always explain to other people that may not understand recovery of an addict. I tell them that the negative behaviors that go along with using drugs will never go away. It is just a matter of choice to use those behaviors to our advantage or not.

Six months after I had returned from my visit, I received a phone call from Shawn telling me to look out for a package in the mail. He was going to send me something that he just knew that I would enjoy, and that I could use.

I asked if it was bigger than a breadbox, and he told me it was not, and that I would just have to wait and see for myself. I had hoped it was nothing sentimental from our visit or some type of expression of thanks. After all, I should have been the one thanking him.

It had been a long ass time that anyone had sent me anything in the mail much less a surprise. For three days, I would come home from work and would break my neck to get to the mailbox to see if this so-called surprise had arrived.

I had no idea of what it could have been, and the anxiety was as if I were a kid waiting for Santa to come down the chimney. While we were together, we shared a lot about our lives and stuff, so I learned a lot about the man that I had not known before.

On the fourth day there it was.

The package was one of those brown mailers to send a CD or photos via mail.

I could not even wait until I got in the house before I tore into it. I opened it in the garage before I got to the door leading into the kitchen.

The contents of that package caught me totally off guard.

To my surprise, what Shawn had sent to me was a six-pack sample of the ED pills that I told him that I was using.

That son of a bitch.

What a guy.

I laughed my ass off at first, and then I just had to call him and ask why he would give up his personal stash of samples and mail all the way to Georgia and leave himself short.

He was not at home when I called, so I left him a message and told him he could not go to bed that night until he called back with an explanation.

When he did call back around 10:30 that evening, he started off with that hearty Shawn laugh that I had come to love over the years.

His answer to my question was simple.

He said, "Easy, I stole them!"

My theory was correct in that he admitted that his trifling ways had not completely left him, when to his benefit.

He told me that when he would go to the doctor for his problems, one of them ED also, the doctor would give him a prescription for pills. He used to get samples just as I did, but he was smart and checked out where the samples were stashed.

When the doctor left the room, good old Shawn would pocket several sample packs, and he had done this on many occasions.

Both of us laughed, and at the same time, I thanked him for looking out for me.

During our weekend visit, as men, we shared the same problems that we were having. We agreed that thank goodness that there was a pill that we could take to continue to have sex with our mates.

Had I not been open and honest, then he would have never known.

Needless to say, these packages kept coming for several months.

There was a time from November of 2005, based on my free samples plus what Shawn was stealing and mailing to me, I had enough to last me eight months.

If Janice is home when Shawn and I are on the phone having our bi-weekly checking in on each other talks, she usually gets on the phone to say hi.

After I had told her about my gifts from him, one evening she got on the phone and asked him jokingly if he was trying to kill her. She told him that she was going to start mailing the packages back so his girlfriend would not get any rest either.

I could hear him laughing on the other end.

No, Janice knew better than to mail back my inventory.

This situation became an avenue of more open and candid dialogue with Janice concerning my ED. Prior to that time I was always so angry talking about the problem that we were having.

I would have never thought that we could make having ED less stressful to deal with prior to her joking with Shawn on the phone.

What I took away from that experience was that it had been the first time that I heard Janice talk to another person about my ED. Doing it in my presence made me realize that this had always been our problem, not just mine.

When Anger Prevents Progress

Timing my intake of the pill also used to be a stressful situation. If I took the dose too early, and we were not in the mood, I would be trying to force the romance. For men, they may think it is okay, but women will tell you in a heartbeat that it is not a turn on.

The fact that the pill had a time restraint attached to it would make me calculate to the hour when would be the ideal time to swallow the pill so that I would get the maximum bang for the buck.

Forgetting for the first four years that I had begun using medications for my ED, I had not spent one nickel.

Instead of this being a blessing, Bruce would still get pissed off if the evening or morning did not result in lovemaking. This was my sick and pessimistic way of saying, "Damn I took the pill for nothing. Shit, I should have saved the dosage for when we were sure that we could seize the moment."

I have since learned that during those times that I felt like that, an attitude such as mine did nothing more than cheapen our relationship. On my part, I was disrespecting Janice to the degree that I had placed an expectation on her for the sake of me being a cheap ass.

A prostitute works on a time frame with their consumer. The meter begins running when money changes hands, and she or he performs whatever the dollar value equates to for the services. Of course, the consumer expects the most for their money, the prostitute expects to give the most for the money, and thus both walk away with a win win situation.

My spouse obviously is not a prostitute, so why was I placing this same form of comparison upon her?

When I understood that this was a selfish, insensitive way to act towards the woman that I love and cherish with all of my heart, I changed my attitude about handling my ED.

Men, you would spend much more on vices that netted you far less rewarding satisfaction. Let us face the facts. It is so true.

We have our big boy toys to play with.

We may enjoy golfing, playing cards on a particular night of the week, fishing, making our cars faster, flat screen televisions, and I can go on.

It would be suffice to say that none of these vices that we drop money on, would bring us the joy and satisfaction of the intimacy that we would enjoy with our mates.

Hell, how often do we go out to dinner and spend $60 and that is not in a fancy restaurant either.

How often do we spend over $100 for concert tickets?

Men, name your vice and you no doubt would not bat an eye spending money on it.

Men, you also would spend much more time kicking yourselves in the ass while living in the "Dog House." I added a wing addition to my "Dog House," as I had spent so many lonely nights there.

When I had hurt Janice's feelings if she was not in the mood, and I had already taken a pill, that was the key to unlock where I would be sleeping that evening.

Men, our mates are actually on our side when it comes to ED.

Therefore, if anything, they are more sensitive to being ready when we are since they understand that our responses are not always due to our own sexual desires for them.

By feeling as though they deliberately turn off the green light in the bedroom, knowing our condition, just cheapens the relationship.

Those feelings that we conjure up in our heads are unfair, disrespectful, and hurtful and most of all takes all of the joy and intimacy out of the act of lovemaking.

I had discovered Bruce's "How to take my pill etiquette" as soon as I was introduced to the pill in 2000. Armed with my newfound discoveries into the wonderful world of ED, I had to modify these etiquettes as I matured.

In the beginning, after my first time taking the pill with Janice's knowledge, I then used to sneak to take my pill. I first would perform the surgery to cut them in half, two to three at a time. I would then place the portions in an empty pill vile.

As of this writing, I still have not invested in one of those pill cutter devices. Just another example of making something easier for me would just take away all of the fun to see how often I can get an even break with my own little thumbs.

Yes, it sounds stupid, but I have not yet said that I was perfect.

Because Friday night for us would still be our date night, I would just always assume that was also the time for making love.

I would forget that there may have been times when Janice would simply want to talk over a glass of wine, and smooth jazz, and just be close without having to feel pressure to getting it on.

She just may have needed to vent about her workweek. On the other hand, she may have wanted to share what she had on her heart and just wanted me to listen.

Listen?

Wow guys, what a novel idea and habit to get into with our mates.

However, for me, this was the evening that I would have to plot out my timing to take the pill.

So right away, I had to calculate my timing to max out the results within the four-hour window of opportunity allowed. This always prevented me from truly listening, because I was so preoccupied with the clock running.

If the evening was not leaning towards sex within three of the four hours, then I would panic that I had just wasted a dosage.

I also would keep the pill in my pocket, look at the clock, figure on how long our conversation would last, and then I would excuse myself and sneak off to take it.

Talk about unnecessary pressure.

I often questioned what happened from the first time that I took the pill with Janice's knowledge to now trying to sneak and hide it.

Pride ran interference with my honesty with my own wife. The very person that if anyone, I should have not kept any secrets from.

That old stubborn pride can be a bitch at times.

I was so proud of the fact that I had overcome my pride when I went to the doctor in the first place.

I was not too puffed up with pride to take the samples and actually use them.

I was not too prideful to share with Janice that I opened up to Dr. Price, Jr about having ED.

Learning To Trust Your Partner

Pride made me crawl back into a black hole, and then try to hide what I was doing from Janice.

Instead of being elated that Janice and I were thrilled with the results, and felt that thank God a solution to a long running problem was within our grasp, I gravitated to my stupid self once again.

I had gone as far as to conjure up my etiquette secretly.

I usually consult with Janice on damn near everything before I do it. After all, that is a solid and necessary ingredient to a good, solid, long lasting relationship.

The frustrations that came along with coming up with these different methods to taking the pill, could have been avoided. If only I had not allowed my stubborn pride to keep Janice out of the mix, together we could have worked out simpler solutions.

I could have avoided a question so often asked by her. When in the middle of just sitting in our family room, sipping some wine, incense burning, and soothing music on the stereo, I would just get up.

Normal question from Janice would then be, "Where are you going?"

Normal answer would be to tell her where I was going right.

No, not me.

I would respond in kind with the same old stupid answer, "Oh I am just getting up."

What kind of stupid answer was "just getting up?"

Hell Janice could see that my ass was just getting up.

Saying that I was just getting up to take care of my business with the pill so that I could really focus on "getting it up," would have been an appropriate answer.

Perhaps Janice sensed that I was not being honest with her since I never could say what I was getting up for. Even if the pill was in my pocket, I just did not have it in me to want to allow Janice to see me taking it.

There had been many occasions while dining in a restaurant that I would excuse myself to go into the men's room to take my pill. Once again, I would gauge how long through desert, paying the check, drive time home, and then settle into the mood. I felt as though I had accomplished something if all this took place inside of 90 minutes.

Whether it was at a party, concert, dinner, of just driving home from work, I would always have to time the moment to take the pill.

That entire extra burden did not make anticipating lovemaking with my lovely and sexy wife, much fun.

The second time that we had taken a cruise was in March 2002.

Our first cruise in February of 2000, remember I was still in denial about having any problems in the hay, and yet we had the time of our lives in every aspect of that first time at sea.

We attributed that pleasant experience in 2000 to both of us being so paranoid and nervous, that we had little time to focus on anything else but having fun.

Since the airport security was still at an all time high right after 9/11 in 2001, the last thing that I had wanted to go through was having my carryon bag being opened with strangers observing my personal shit.

Therefore, I just packed the pills in the same vile as my blood pressure pills, and my vitamins and herbs.

I did not want to calculate in my brain just how many to take, so I just bought the entire six-pack of sample. Who gave a gnat's ass if they were not used and had to bring them back home.

This theory put less pressure on both of us that if we did not use, we would lose.

What I had discovered on the second cruise, was that during the day, you are out in the sun, and doing shore excursions.

Then it was racing back to the ship so your ass would not be left having everyone on deck waving your ass goodbye.

After showering and getting dressed for dinner, then the theater would open for the evening show, and then of course play the slots for 15 to 20 minutes. By the time you got back to your cabin, you were dead to the world.

Therefore, the notion that five nights at sea equated to five nights of romance simply was not true. It would be a miracle if you mustered up the energy in the morning before the day's activities.

This became a challenge for me because I could not gauge when to take the pill.

On the other hand, we had so much fun, it did not matter much.

Several evenings resulted in both of us falling to sleep to the motion of the ship.

Now I could forget trying to nudge my darling wife in the early morning on a cruise.

You know that nudge guys.

The nudge that indicates in our minds, a time for romance before we begin our day.

I love to awake early.

So on this cruise, I wanted Janice to awake early with me in order to stand at the bow of the ship, and watch the sunrise as we pulled into port.

I did not mean every morning, just the first morning.

In my opinion, this was so romantic, and no different from holding hands on deck in the moonlight.

On the other hand, Janice had her own ideas that usually won out.

I ended up standing on the bow that first morning, cup of coffee in hand, and striking up a conversation with another man whose wife said to him, "Screw you. I aint getting up early on vacation to see no sun rise."

So the two of us ended up talking shit, and watched the sunrise as the ship jockeyed into port. Then we said our goodbyes, and went back to wake our wives to begin getting ready to go ashore.

Seven cruises later, Janice had promised me that one morning she would get up an experience that romantic moment with me.

We just took our fourteenth cruise in April of 2009, and I am still waiting!

Looking back in hindsight, I realized that as much as I was trying to keep my method of taking my pill a secret from Janice, all along she was giving me more ideas to add to my etiquette portfolio, only she did not know it.

What to do for a morning tryst was another challenge that I had learned to overcome.

It is no secret that many ED suffers have no problem in getting an erection. However, to be able to have one and keep one when we want one, now there lay the frustrations.

I would have absolutely no problem waking up in the middle of the night or early morning with an erection.

What would prevent me from attempting to do that manly nudge to accidently on purpose wake Janice up?

The answer is that if I tried for a little "something something" in the wee hours or early morning, more often than not, my penis friend would fall back to sleep on us. Now that my fellow man is the ultimate of frustrations.

Watching or feeling your erection going bye-bye and there aint shit that you can do about it really sucks.

Rather than face embarrassment, I would sneak down the hall to my inner sanctum called my office.

There I would go to my top dresser drawer in the closet, (yes Janice has the entire master closet to herself, and I am down the hall with 15 hangers of my stuff) and pop a pill.

I would then sneak back down the hall, crawl back under the covers, and await a miracle to unfold.

That particular etiquette I hated the most.

Bruce's usual irrational reasoning, or as Janice calls it, "Bruce's laws," was that why should I have to waste a pill when I should have been able to utilize my natural hard on.

I mean if an erection came along, then before I could use it, bingo, back to its natural limp state, I felt that was unfair.

I would begin that ridiculous conversation with my penis again as to why it could not just stay at attention for a least another fifteen minutes or so.

Thus, I could have saved a dosage for a time better spent.

Nevertheless, the urge to splurge was stronger than the need to be cheap.

So at times like those, I used to just go ahead and say, "Fuck it! Tomorrow was promised to no one so make hay while the sun shines."

The decision to start making my taking the pill a joke amongst Janice and me was a major hurdle in the right direction in avoiding that feeling of failure in me.

By involving Janice in the entire process of this adjustment in our personal lives, was how it should have been from day one. Hiding out as I used to call it, did very little for my ego.

Keeping my pill consumption methods from Janice was like a child sneaking behind a parent's back to avoid being caught.

What would the consequences have been for a husband that was busted taking a pill that his doctor had prescribed to enhance the intimacy in his marriage?

What would a partner do to the one who was doing all that was necessary, to ensure that the romance in their lives would not flicker away and die?

I had no clue as to the answers to these questions in the beginning of my acceptance that I was an ED sufferer. I did not have time to wonder about situations that would have made me feel worse than I was already feeling.

Often times I would curse out God for having to put me through the humiliation, and additional work for a natural process.

In my mind, I felt as though a gift from God in the form of lovemaking should not have had to be marred by ED, and pills.

I know that sounds childish, and so non-Christian like. However, I am convinced that God sees many of his children shake their fists up to Him in anger, and ask that 64-thousand dollar question of, WHY ME LORD?

I am equally convinced that God replies, "If not you fool, then who?"

Many a comic will tell you that laughter is so much better than crying. The majority of comedians begin their careers based on their personal life experiences that at the time may have bought sadness into their lives.

As a result, they turn their unpleasant situations into routines that bring forth laugher to the faces of many. This becomes a win win situation.

When a person can laugh at himself or herself, then they can begin to move on and not place so much value on the things that made them sad.

I had wanted to get to that place with my ED.

I wanted to laugh about it.

I wanted to talk openly about it.

I wanted to write about it.

I wanted to learn more about it.

I wanted to control it, rather than it controlling me.

Can All Of These Pills Be For Real?

Moving right along into 2002, more research, and resources had been given by the other pharmaceutical companies to jump on the bandwagon. The race was on by competitors for a new and improved solution to combat ED.

I remembered watching television one evening in August of 2002, when I caught the tail ending of a commercial. I would always catch the ending of any commercial because I would change the channel. I refused to watch any of them.

Well, there was this one particular commercial showing this middle age couple, walking through the woods hand and hand and all lovey dovey. The visual was nice. However, it was the words that I had heard that really got my attention.

The deep manly voice in the commercial said, "And could last up to 36 hours."

Did I hear correctly?

Thirty-six long hours?

One whole 24-hour day plus another12 hours?

I kept repeating these questions over and over for about twenty minutes.

The same commercial showed again that evening. This time I damn sure paid attention to the words.

I was so proud of myself for not turning it off.

That commercial was advertising for another new wonder pill for ED. The difference with this one pill in particular could allow you to be ready when the moment was right.

Wow!

What an awesome slogan. Would this mean that I did not have to rack my brain planning the timing for taking the pill? Would this mean that I would no longer have to set the timer for the four hour timeframe?

I had heard correctly from the first initial time I saw the commercial. What had made this new pill so incredible was the fact that it was the first and only one to last up to thirty-six hours.

"Shit, what a breakthrough for men" I told myself.

Then out came the skepticism in my sorry ass.

This could not really be happening in my lifetime.

The saying, "If it sounds too good to be true, it probably is" came to mind.

Could this pill actually perform in the fashion that the company is advertising that it could?

If so, then what a major breakthrough.

My next thought was unselfish.

I thought that hell, if this pill did work as the ad said that it would, think of all the couples suffering from ED that could benefit.

I thought of all the couples that would be ecstatic not having to be pressured into just trying to squeeze in the intimacy into four hours or less.

Live long enough and wonders do happen.

Now if you guessed my next move, you guessed correctly.

My next step just after seeing the commercial in its entirety was that I just had to ask Dr. Price, Jr to let me try it.

I am for sure that the manufactures reps were out in doctor's offices the day that their thirty-six hour long lasting pill hit the marketplace. I was for damn certain that I would be one of the first on line.

I made one of my unnecessary appointments for something minor just to get in to see him.

I had just had my annual physical that June so he had already given me my prescription for a yearly supply of the current pill. Along with my usual two six packs of samples, I was good to go.

However, this trip to him was more important than what he already prescribed.

This visit meant that I could also jump on the gravy train with other men that can take a pill and last up to 36 hours.

What a miraculous discovery, and surely another victory for us ED sufferers.

I had begun a new job in July of 2002.

I immediately became very close with a young Black woman by the name of Rosalind. Along with a male manager, he and Rosalind actually interviewed me for the position.

For some reason I was very grateful for her assistance in guiding me through the interview process. I was even more grateful that I was offered the job the next day.

Grateful was an understatement as my unemployment benefits were running out the week prior to my starting the new job.

When you add a lack of finances to your marriage or any relationship, add the fact that your manhood aint working right, it is a formula for disaster. Whomever penned the phrase, "aint no romance without no finance," was right on the money.

It had not taken me long to fit right in with the current employees. The company was very small and intimate, so getting to know everyone and they getting to know me were quite a simple process.

Rosalind held the position as Trainer for the new hires, and when she was not training employees, she was assigned another function. Her role outside of the training room had kept her in a cubicle most of the day monitoring our phone calls for quality assurance.

I used to think it to be a lonely existence not interacting with others, but she did not seem to mind at all.

She would call me into her cubicle from time to time, as she did the other eight Customer Service representatives. I hated listening to myself on the phone, but had no choice.

My calls used to amuse her. I always had a funny way of talking to the clients to diffuse any negative issues that they may have had. However, she did notice a pattern of me being somewhat gruff on the calls that I had taken prior to 9 o'clock in the morning.

I had not realized that when I went into the office at 8 a.m. when I was pissed off, I was taking my frustrations out on the first person on the opposite end of the telephone.

Was that the right thing to do?

Of course not.

However, I had never heard myself being so condescending on the phone to anyone before. I mean I was just about telling the customers to go screw themselves.

Rosalind once told me that her favorite Bruce saying when I was in a piss poor mood was, "Now hear me and hear me well."

That was like telling a customer to shut up, and listen to what I had to say. Not me listening to what their needs were or what they had to say.

We all know that I could have lost my job for that type of behavior.

My visits into Rosalind's cubicle became more frequent than for anyone else due to this issue with my attitude.

Naturally, she was not aware of the root cause of my anger and frustrations. Many a morning anger for me was a carryover from a night prior of being frustrated in the lovemaking department.

It was not an uncommon occurrence to attempt lovemaking during a weeknight, which often caused me to remain pissed off the next morning if my dick had not worked.

Now I would never had just come out and said, "You know Rosalind, the reason I sound so angry many times on the phone in the morning is because I have ED."

Although it was the truth, I had just met the person who had been so nice to me from day one. I felt that sharing something so very personal was not appropriate.

Therefore, I just had to offer excuse after excuse for my negative phone etiquette.

Well that shit only lasted for about 60 days.

When my ass was threatened to be written up unless I changed my tone of voice and lack of professionalism on the phone, I changed very quickly.

Gradually our little one on one meeting turned into conversations on subjects outside of the job functions. We began to discuss family, relationships, careers, likes and dislikes, and most of all that we felt that we could and should be doing better than what we were doing work wise.

I respected her honesty and life experiences for such a young woman of only 30 yrs old. We then began to share more of ourselves, and felt even more comfortable that neither of us would do anything to jeopardize that relationship.

She soon dubbed herself as "the daughter that I never had."

She had accepted an invitation to our home for our annual Christmas tree decorating party that year. We had to keep the fraternizing hush hush as God forbid that a co-worker found out that we socialized outside of work.

Sadly, too often relationships between men and women at work can result in an extra marital affair. Even if the relationship is just on a friend's level, co-workers with little to nothing to do with their lives will assume that a sexual thing is going on.

My main concern in this situation was that certain pain in the ass co-workers would want to ask me why they had not been invited.

About a month after Rosalind attended our Christmas party, I busted her sitting at her desk looking at a website for singles. At first, she was somewhat embarrassed.

However, that was the turning point in our relationship of our being more open and honest on subjects pertaining to our personal lives.

I had learned that she was once engaged to an airline pilot. She had dated both Black and White men. She was somewhat anxious to get married and have a child before her biological clock stopped ticking. She wanted to return to college. She also hated her job.

Once she opened up for me to know her better, she was no different from most females that had the opportunity to ask a married man the loaded question. That question was, "What is the secret to a successful marriage?"

Knowing that I had been married 30 years, as long as was her age, she was awe struck to have met a Black couple married that long. When she met Janice at our house, she observed that not only were we married a long time, but we showed the love also.

Unlike the answer that I would always give to someone, for some reason I had felt that she deserved a better answer than my canned answer to people. That answer was the same old "communication and not going to bed angry bullshit."

For Rosalind, I pushed the envelope somewhat, as I had felt that she could handle my honesty. She was such a mature 30 years old, and I had no doubts that she would ever go blabbing my business all over the office.

What I shared with her was that couples always need to keep their marriage alive by not only communicating, but also romance and intimacy was mandatory.

Money of course is important also, but it should never be number one or number two on the priority wheel of your lives as one.

I opened up and talked about ED, and the problems that many men experience. I explained that men go through this situation, and it could take its toll in a relationship.

At first Rosalind just looked at me in shock that although we were beginning to share more of ourselves, I would brooch a subject so sensitive.

When I began talking about the wonder pill of the century, she could tell from my enthusiasm as I spoke that I must have tried it. She asked me anyway just to erase any doubt in her mind if I had tried the pill. I answered that I had.

She then asked, "Well did it work?" I just smiled and she knew the answer.

Being true to my word, I answered several more of her questions in the area of intimacy as though it was not a big deal. She was amazed that she would be able to ask honest questions, especially to a man, and actually receive honest answers.

For Bruce, what the response from Rosalind showed me was that it was okay to discuss ED in the presence of another female other than your significant other.

I felt very comfortable in sharing the truth, and what that did for me was admitting that this topic about ED should be shared.

My 19-year-old nephew named Jason, had a gig at a drugstore in the summer of 2008. He has such a funny way of telling a story. He had no reason to fabricate any part of what he had ever experienced, which was a good quality in a young person.

He worked the check out register, as he was too young to work in the pharmacy.

One evening in June of that year, he said that a man in his thirties came up to his register to pay for his prescription. Being new, Jason could not find the price sticker code on the little bag. Being the responsible employee that he was raised to be, he simply picked up the intercom to call over the assistant manager to do a price check.

Jason said that the man got livid.

He began to call him out by saying that he deliberately embarrassed him by calling over the assistant manager. The man felt that Jason should have left his register to go back to the pharmacy to check the price himself.

Even though he explained that he was not allowed to leave his register unattended, and if would just be a few seconds for this issue to be resolved, the man still was fuming.

Why was this thirty something male customer so irate?

Number one, his prescription was for the wonder pills.

Number two, the assistant manager was a female.

Number three, the pharmacist was a female, which is why he did not want to ring up the purchase in the pharmacy. How stupid to think it to be a secret when she filled the prescription in the first place.

I asked my nephew what was the outcome to this scenario. He told me that the man left without his prescription. The man allowed his pride and stereotype of ED sufferers to prevent him from getting his dosage to help with his problem.

I laughed with Jason about his experience, but I would not have laughed seven years prior to that.

I was nervous as hell because by 2003, there was now a third pill that took the ED population by storm. This pill came out six months after the 36-hour pill was introduced. However, I was not sure what was so special about it.

The fact that it did not boast that it could last up to 36 hours, which that in itself lead me to dismiss the latest pill as not to be too high on my list. In addition, the side effects based on their advertisement did little to peak my curiosity to try it.

My physical in July of 2004, netted me a new prescription for each of the three ED medications. I was advised to add the latest one to experience for myself the results, and not to rely too heavily on what I heard or saw on the television commercials.

The original pill that I began in 2000 was still my safety net. I had trusted that baby for four long years. Then in 2002, I experienced the 36-hour pill, so why begin to experiment with something new on the market.

"If it aint broke, don't fix it," as the saying goes.

Since Dr. Price, Jr knew that I was a cheap ass, he had arranged to give me free coupons. These coupons when attached to a first time prescription, would entitle you to a free trial of three pills.

Because now what we had were the big three pharmaceutical companies all vying for an equal or majority share of the marketplace. They assumed that if you were willing to at least sample their product and liked it, then they would have you for life.

Hell, I figured what had I to lose. I was made an offer that I could not refuse. With prescriptions in hand, I went to three different pharmacies to place my free sample scripts.

I was loyal to my two regular pharmacists, Dan, or Virgil though. I felt comfortable with each to know my business. Since I had filled the original pill with them, I had to place one of the newer ones there. The coupons had to be a first time prescription.

I made it a point to try two other locations for the other two prescriptions. Of course, I made certain that each had male pharmacists.

When I went back to the second choice pharmacy to pick up my prescription for the 36-hour long pill, I was pleasantly surprised. The pharmacist's assistant turned out to be a member of our church.

I attempted to duck down an aisle because I was embarrassed to have her know that I was having problems with my dick.

Eventually, I did return to pick up my three pills, but it took me a month to do it. In addition, oh yes, I made certain that she was not on duty.

For my personal results, I must say that all three worked well.

The 36-hour pill has to be at the top of my list when it comes to rekindling the spontaneity in our love life.

I would like to speak on men viewing pornography.

Should men use this method of stimulation to substitute for taking a pill to get an erection?

Should partners accept this method when their man brings this form of arousal into the bedroom?

Should it matter which method is used as long as the results are the same?

Should men justify the costs of renting a pornographic DVD as cheaper than paying $42-$48 for a few ED pills?

Think about the psychological affect that using pornography as a substitute for stimulating yourself has on your partner.

I have often viewed the use of pornography as a personal choice. That applies to both men and women.

Too many other issues of a larger magnitude need to be addressed instead of worrying if a couple are in the privacy of their own home watching a porn DVD.

Now this is just my opinion.

If a couple having difficulty in conceiving and the woman exhausted all of her methods of being checked for deficiencies, what is usually the next step? The next step is the poor man has to go and have his sperm counted from a sample of his semen.

How does the sample get into the little laboratory cup with the lid on it?

The man goes to the doctor's office. He is handed the cup and lid, usually by whom?

A female assistant or nurse.

Next, he is instructed to go into a room all by his lonesome. Then he watches a porn DVD to get aroused and masturbates until he has his sample.

Is this not socially acceptable?

Is the man looked upon as a pervert?

Is the man cheapening his marriage any by doing this process?

Did the process bring forth the necessary results?

Since I do not want to elaborate too much on this subject, I will leave those questions in the hands of the reader to answer.

So why bring up the subject?

The only reason is this is a reality that men do explore.

Watching pornography may be easier than discussing ED with a partner, a doctor, another man or admitting that help is needed.

Now if this is what a man elects to do to substitute taking medications, then a strong suggestion is to question why the resistance to seeking alternative methods to achieve an erection.

Just like with medications, watching pornography can become an addictive behavior.

However, there is a much better reason not to resort to this option.

Think about your partner's feelings if you are found to be using porn to enhance your getting an erection.

I may be wrong, but I feel that a partner would much more respect the decision for her man to talk to his doctor, take a pill, and then let the intimacy flow.

Just my opinion.

I had encountered the most unusual situation while flying back from Miami to Atlanta in November of 2006.

I was returning from Montego Bay, Jamaica, with five of my co-workers after spending four luxurious nights in two of the most beautiful, beachfront, five-star resorts that I had ever experienced.

This was a business trip for my job as a travel agent, so it was not as though I was there for romantic reasons. In total, there were 15 travel agents from different parts of the United States.

During those five days, it was pure fun, sun, and being treated as if we were big ballers and shot callers. The purpose was to experience how the other half lived. As travel agents, we were expected to return to our jobs, and advise which wonderful places our clients should stay.

Well, by the second day, I was sick and tired of listening to our chaperone and three other agents sharing their individual experiences with gastric bypass surgeries.

I mean it was not too bad while on the tour bus, or around the bar in the evening. However, I found it a bit disgusting listening to them talk about their surgeries during meal times.

To each his own, but respect for other people's feelings that cared to not wish to be part of their conversation should have been a priority.

My opinion of our male chaperone, Walter, became biased to the point of me feeling as though he was a royal pain in the ass. Therefore, human nature would have me to try to avoid any conversation with him the remainder of the trip.

How ironic that we ended up sitting together on our flight back from Miami to Atlanta. God forbid our company not save a buck and allow us to fly nonstop. However, hey, it was free, so layover or not, I would never have gotten the opportunity to experience being treated like a king.

I had no choice but to strike up a conversation with him.

I am nervous as hell when it comes to flying to begin with, so even if he were a stranger a conversation would have taken place. I would have seen to that.

My biggest fear that I have yet to overcome is the take off.

I hate that part of flying the most.

Somehow, it just defies the law of gravity for a ton of metal, loaded with over 200 people, fuel, luggage and cargo to lift off the ground and keep on getting up.

Before we even taxied from the gate, I had broken the ice by sharing that I had written a book about my life, and was proud of that accomplishment. I did not go into much detail other than the title, "Full Circle – From Addiction to Affection."

I suggested that if he was interested to order online, and I that I would even autograph for him since we worked in the same office.

He then had asked if I had plans in the future to pen another book, and I thought for a moment before I had answered. I thought at first, as I was embarrassed. Unlike my other co-worker, Rosalind, I had not known Walter like that, to put my business out there just yet.

I did reply that I was in the process of writing another book.

I was preparing myself for the next question from him, which was obviously, "What is your new book about?"

"What the hell," I thought to myself. "Might just as well go on and tell him."

Without any further delays, I simply answered, "Erectile dysfunction."

To my surprise, Walter appeared not to be phased in the least with my response. In fact, he sat up straight in his seat, and replied that he found that to be interesting.

Now when Walter first began working in our office only four months prior to our trip, it was obvious to me that he was gay. However, in the travel industry, that was not unusual

For the first of many times that I had flown, talking to Walter prevented me from having my nose glued to the window by my seat. I mean the kid here had his ears open listening to any strange noises. I watched the ground crew to make sure they put fuel in the plane, closed the baggage doors, and that the co-pilot did his/her walk around the plane.

Of course, everyone has a bad day at work, so I just wanted to be sure that the crew were on top of my flight concerning safety.

Walter and I continued talking, and I was not even paying attention as the plane roared down the runway and lifted off into the wild blue yonder. That was a first as not even Janice could keep my mind off the part of flying that I despised the most.

Why had Walter grabbed hold of my attention to the point that it took my mind off the takeoff?

He shared with me that he also suffered from ED, and he was only 33 years old.

Now that really blew me away.

I had never had a young, gay, Black, male share anything so personal with me before. Of course, it is not a secret that I know many men that fit his criteria. Never the less, I found talking to Walter fascinating.

We talked nonstop the entire one hour and twenty-three minute flight. He shared that he felt that his ED was a direct result of his obesity. Since his storytelling during our trip grossed me out, I had not listened to him sharing how he at one time weighed 350 pounds.

He had lost a total of 95 pounds at that time as a result of the surgery.

It then became apparent to me why during our Dolphin encounter, and beach time, that Walter always wore a tank top. He must have been embarrassed as his arms, and upper body was not toned.

I felt it okay to open up further and ask which of the three pills on the market he preferred the best.

When he told me which his preference was, I grimaced. The very one which gave him the best results, was the one that gave me the worse headache. It worked when I took the free trial samples, but my goodness, the next morning was a bitch.

On the other hand, he did not enjoy the two that I found to be the best for me.

Thus, that is why options are given. What works for one, may not work for the other.

Wow!

For the first time, I actually opened up to another man that I did not really know that well about ED. The results were enlightening.

What I learned from that encounter was that ED does affect men much younger than me.

Somehow reading about the statistics and actually having a man talk to you in person about this subject adds another dimension.

Walter may have been honest regards to his ED. However, he was not honest with his employer so I soon found out.

Just two short weeks after our return from Jamaica, he left one day from the office, and I had not seen him since. Of course, rumors had it that he hauled ass before he was fired for poor job performance. Who knows for sure.

I was just disappointed to not be able to talk with him more to gather more information for my writings.

He had promised to hook me up with others that he had known to add more knowledge for my book. This would have opened up a new avenue into the lives of gay men suffering from ED.

I actually believed he would be true to his word. However, he must have had some other negative issues going on in his life at the time.

A Few Setbacks Along The Way

The moment that I had dreaded finally arrived.

During the spring of 2007, I had noticed that the response from taking half of a 50 mg tablet was not giving the old boy here that same gusto of earlier years.

The time came that I used to always question. In the back of my little brain, I would often ask the question, "Damn. What if the pill no longer worked for me?"

I had become so overly confident in the ability of the pill that the very thought of it not working gave a false sense of security. I have often heard that a person's body can build up a tolerance for frequently used medications.

Since Janice would always be aware of the results factor, it was not a big mystery to me that she realized too that the erections were not the best. Would she mention anything to me?

Of course, she would. Why would she not?

I firmly emphasize the importance in communicating between couples. By her not saying anything would only cause all of our hard working through my ED condition, to resort back to our beginning. That is a place that we never would want to visit again.

She understood that pretending to not notice was unfair to both of us.

Had I not responded in a positive manner would also have been unfair.

We just accepted this as just another part of our 37 years together, and that this too shall pass.

April 14, 2007, our planned seven night cruise was about to begin.

I had been sick with a very bad chest cold, and cough just 10 days prior. The condition had kept me out of work for three days. I hated using sick time at work for being sick. I always felt that time should be used when one just did not feel like going to work.

By April 11, I was becoming quite alarmed to the point of opting to cancel the cruise. With our cruise insurance, we would get a refund. However, the plane tickets to San Juan from Atlanta would be an issue.

Me being an asthmatic, I took Mom's advice and went to visit a pulmonary specialist on the 12th. Nothing that Dr. Price, Jr had given me seemed to be working. I needed the specialist to prescribe anything to make the cough go away, in less than 48 hours.

Suffice to say, whatever he had given me I took it in the parking lot of the pharmacy. I did not even worry to read the side affects. He had prescribed two different pills.

This was crunch time and no time to be paranoid and all. This was a dire emergency. Too much work and planning had gone into making this cruise our best, and Lord knows we needed to vacation in a bad way.

Add in the fact that I lucked out and got the last outside cabin, our vacation time approved well in advance, and cheap airfare.

No way was I going to miss this.

I began taking this tablet that included Codeine for the cough. My fear of any narcotic was not an issue. However, I had noticed that it made me kind of out of sorts.

This could have just been my own anxiety. Regardless I continued the dosages, because the results were amazing. I still had a cough, but not to the degree as before.

By the time that we had boarded the plane to San Juan to meet the ship, I felt as if I was stoned. This was not a good feeling for an ex-drug addict.

As I mentioned in an earlier chapter, flying was not my most favorite pastime. In spite of my nervous nature, once we took off, I actually curled up in three empty seats together with a blanket and pillow and went to sleep. I knew that I had to be out of it to do that.

I still was not out of the woods completely with the coughing, but the two and a half hours of sleep did me some good.

We were able to board the ship nine hours prior to the 10 o'clock in the evening sailing time. This allowed us time to settle in, eat lunch, and just enjoy the ship even though we were still in port.

We had learned from prior cruises to pack our bathing suits in our carry on. Often times it may take hours before you ever see your luggage.

I changed, and sat in the sun thinking that would help my cold and coughing.

When I awoke from another nap, I had noticed that I was still feeling somewhat weird. My paranoia set in and I began to think that I would hate to be out to sea and have something go wrong with me.

I had decided immediately to screw taking anymore of the cough pills. I would rather continue to cough, than to feel the way that I was feeling.

As quiet as it is kept, I was more concerned that those pills would interfere with the one pill that really mattered on this cruise. The pill that counted the most was at stake.

I locked the two prescriptions in the safe, and did not touch them until I returned home eight days later. I knew that I had to sacrifice one or the others, so guess which pill won.

We showered, got dressed for the informal dinner, then the entertainment for the evening.

My own protocol for taking my 25 mg pill on a cruise was at least by 7 o'clock in the evening. This was just in the event the occasion called for intimacy. Usually from a day of traveling, and time change, we both would be too tired for anything but a good night sleep. However, wonders do happen less I not be prepared.

That evening is when I realized for sure that my trusted little pill that had been my best friend for seven years, had let me down.

I mean really down.

Of course, Bruce should have chalked it up to perhaps a combination of so many other drugs that were in my system. This may have prevented the pill from doing what it had been doing so faithfully up until then.

Throw in the fact that we both were tired, yet tried to engage in lovemaking anyway.

Those factors created a disappointing evening to say the least.

In addition, yes, I will not lie, for a brief moment I was pissed off. I tried not to show it in front of Janice. She then simply just kissed me goodnight without saying a word. That was her way of soothing my disappointment that time.

I can say most proudly, is that I was not letting my disappointment linger. As quickly as I felt it coming on, I just laid back, held Janice, and was thankful to have made the trip in the first place.

Therefore, off to beddy-bye we went, and we were both out for the count within minutes.

The next morning I awoke feeling so much more energetic, and not as lethargic as the days prior. I was certain that the lack of medications was the reason.

By the time we disembarked at our first port of call in St. Thomas, I still had a bad coughing spell while walking in town. It scared the shit out of me. Janice bless her heart was just hoping that I did not cough myself to death before she could finish her favorite pastime – shopping!

On a previous visit to St Thomas four years earlier, we had lunch at a small local restaurant. It was down an alley was all that we had remembered, but we found it. The woman that owned it was famous for her hot sauces.

I had no appetite, but she recommended an herbal tea.

Until this day, I do not know what she had put in it, but after drinking it that afternoon, I never coughed again for the duration of the cruise. There is something to be said for old fashion remedies from the Caribbean. I was so thankful.

I decided to up my dosage to taking the whole 50 mg tablet for the ED. Why would I want to leave room for any disappointments? I had packed extra so what was the point in playing Russian roulette with our intimacy.

Maybe it was all the other medications, and maybe it was just time to up the dosage. At the time, I did not really care to analyze the reasons. All I know was that it turned out to be the best cruise that we had ever had in many ways.

Therefore, it was then that I had accepted the fact that it was time for me to stop playing nickel and dime with what was such an important aspect of our marriage.

When I returned from our April cruise, I was not in need of any samples for at least two months. I placed a call to Sarah around the first week of June. I never like to leave to chance that I may run out.

I thought nothing of the same scenario that I had been a part of for the past seven years. That was just walking into the office, saying hi, asking if my bag of samples were ready, and thanking the receptionist and leaving.

On this particular day, I had three stops to make during my weekday off, which was always on Tuesdays.

At first, I did not plan to make Dr. Price, Jr's office one of my stops. However, after my normal routine of changing my mind a half dozen times, I decided why not. I usually do not even have to turn off my car. That is how quickly I would be in and out.

This day, I turned off the car for some reason.

When I went in, the waiting room was empty except for one Black man sitting there. I could tell that he was a pharmaceutical representative, just by his dress, and a dead giveaway was his sample suitcase. You know the one with the wheels and extendable handle.

I went up to the desk and asked my normal question, "Did Sarah leave anything in the sample bin for me?"

The regular staff member was not on duty. However, I had asked Doris, who had been working there for past 15 years, if she could check. She went under the counter and searched only to reply that she had not seen any bags with my name on it.

Something told me to just leave it alone, and just say good-bye, and that I would just call Sarah later. This was not the first time that Sarah had not responded to my voice message, so it was no big deal. After all, she was doing me a favor, so I had no reason to get an attitude over it. In addition, I was not completely out of everything anyway.

Here again for the God only knows how many times I have done this, I changed my mind. Instead of taking my ass and leaving, I had to push the envelope.

Another staff member name Karla, who had just gotten married, just happened to come up to the reception counter. The other three staff members were just talking since it was not busy that day.

Karla usually is the technician that takes your blood pressures, lab work, and vitals when you arrive. Prior to leading you to the examining room, she and I often would engage in conversation. In addition, she was young and very attractive, but a little ditzy.

Karla had been employed for no more than five years, and by far the youngest staff member. Therefore, it was not as though I would have expected what was to come next.

I politely asked her how the wedding went, and she came over to show off her ring and brag about her big day.

During that exchange of conversation, Doris in the meantime asked me what samples I had needed. She offered to go in the back and fill my request.

Once again, my mind told me to just leave, since I had another stop to make anyway. However, no not me. I had to hold my hand to one side of my face and whisper to Doris what I came for.

Karla with her nosey ass overheard what I was asking for. She then proceeded to make a complete spectacle of the entire situation. She proceeded to talk loud enough for everyone including the sales rep to hear.

I was shocked. I just stood there like and asshole in disbelief. I just looked at her and said, "Gee Karla, just tell everyone my personal business."

I felt that she would get the hint. Forgetting she was young, immature, and on top of everything else, an airhead at times.

She then asked aloud how many milligrams I usually get, and which pill I preferred, and she would personally go in the storeroom and check for me.

I was so embarrassed.

I could not believe my ears, and eyes, how unprofessional her behavior was.

Of course, it is no secret to the office as to what all of my medications were, including free samples. Each one is listed clearly on my chart, so that was not the reason for my feeling embarrassed.

It was almost as if she was deliberately trying to humiliate me. Why, I will never know.

Rather than waiting for her to return, I should have just left and saved the little bit of dignity I had left.

Doris and the other three staff members looked at me in such shock. Their expressions all reflected a sense of embarrassment for me as well. After all, after close to 20 years as a patient and most of them had been there just as long, we were like family.

I felt that if I had just left, I would have admitted that I was making a big deal over her behavior. So I just stood there and talked to Doris about me writing a book on the subject of men with ED. She then proceeded to share with me about her husband leaving her and her two teenage daughters after 22 years of marriage.

I was trying to keep my cool. I did not want to say to her that I really did not give two shits about her problems. I listened, offered my empathy, and some pearls of wisdom as she moved on with her life.

Of course, it seemed as though it took forever for Karla to come back to the front, which made me even more pissed off.

After what felt like all of 15 minutes, she comes out grinning. She then announced in her loud voice that all that was available was one six pack of 50 mg, and that the other two alternate products were not in stock.

She then just nonchalantly handed the pack over the counter to me, no bag or anything and said grinning, "Here you go. Hope it helps!"

By this time, I glanced over to the sales rep, who was peering over the top of the magazine that he was reading. He must have been saying, "I have never witnessed anything so unprofessional in my life."

I had no choice by then but to accept the samples since I had waited. After going t through all that shit, I would have looked more like an idiot had I declined.

All the while, she had no idea just how close she came to me leaning over the counter and slapping that shit ass-eating grin off her face.

How dare her disrespect a patient like that. Especially when that patient was me.

When I had left, I had just chalked it up to just another funny chapter in the life and times of Bruce Codrington. The first person that I called when I got back in my car on my way to my last stop of the day was my man Joe.

I told Joe the story of what happened with a sense of humor in order to diffuse my anger and humiliated feelings. He had laughed but reiterated that she was completely out of line.

Well, by the time that I had spoken to a third friend about it two hours later, it was no longer a laughing matter. Something came over my spirit, and I became very angry. I think it was like an afterthought that we all experience.

Have you ever been in a situation, handled it one way, and then later on you want to kick yourself in the ass?

What happens is you are playing repeatedly in your mind what you should have could have done differently. Of course, hindsight is always 2020 vision, and truth is given the same situation, you would do the same damn thing anyway.

It is normal to look back, but what is not normal, is letting the situation go without at least trying to make amends. It is a pride thing also.

Therefore, my next call was not to another friend, or even Janice who I elected not to bother her with this.

No, my next call before the office closed was to Sarah to share with her what had happened. I knew that I had to leave a voice message for her, and I made damn certain that it was very detailed. The more detailed that I became, the angrier that I got, so I just ended the call.

The next thing that I did when I returned home that afternoon, was to write a two-page letter to Dr. Price, Jr to tell him I was too embarrassed to ever come back as a patient.

Janice and I had our annual physicals scheduled for that July 31, and I even went as far as to requesting him to cancel mine.

In the midst of writing my letter, Sarah called me back. She was so apologetic on the phone, and asked that I do not consider this incident to keep me from returning.

She admitted that her behavior was uncalled for. She also said that the other staff members had told her how shocked that they were at Karla's behavior.

When I got around to sharing with Janice that evening what had happened, she felt I was overreacting. She went further and explained that trying to find another doctor that was like Dr. Price, Jr would be very difficult if not impossible.

She said, he and everyone else had been nothing less than like family to us. It would be unfair to let one asshole, ruin a family relationship. Once again, Janice was right. I could never recreate a doctor patient relationship like I had with Dr. Price, Jr so why even try.

Two days later, I received a letter in the mail. It was from Karla. She wrote to apologize for her actions, and said she did not intend to embarrass me. She said how badly she felt afterwards when she heard that I had called to threaten to leave as a patient.

What else could I do but to keep my appointment of July 31, and let bygones be bygones.

To show how our doctor patient relationship is so strong, the first order of business when I sat down with Dr. Price, Jr was the situation with Karla. He did not want to not address it.

He first thanked me for bringing it to his attention. Had I not, he would never have known how I felt. He also told me that Karla was spoken to by him, and that she cried, and apologized, as she meant no harm. It was her idea he said for her to write me a letter.

I felt that her intent to ask for forgiveness was not something that she was made to do by her boss, but from her.

Up until today, she will not have any contact with me. I say hello when I see her, but nothing more. She once even asked another technician to draw my blood, when I went for an office visit.

I guess she felt that if she hurt me, I would think that she was trying to be vindictive.

How this incident relates to ED is that even after seven years of living with ED at that time, I still became embarrassed.

I had been talking more openly about ED. I had even come up with the idea to write a book about my personal experiences. Yet and still, I allowed this person to strike a sensitive nerve regarding the subject.

Even though I had come to grips with acceptance, the problem still touches a chord when it comes to my masculinity. That connection between the two issues is why I still get very defensive.

Because Janice usually schedules her appointment 45 minutes before me, we always pass each other in the hall and joke with each other.

Another reason that Janice goes in first is so she can talk to the doctor about me and my issues. She knows that most men do not tell their doctors everything that is bothering them. She is right in that respect. It must be a man thing.

He always talks to me about what Janice talks to him about concerning my health. Of course, he always obtains Janice's permission to discuss her concerns about me with me, so no secrets are kept.

On this visit, Janice shared with him that I still get pissed off when the pill may not work sometimes. In addition, I get so worked up with anxiety, she feels that psychologically I set myself up for failure before I even allow the pill to work.

These are valid points that she made to him. She was also correct that I would not bring up the issue, so that is why she did.

That is the type of relationship we all have. I value that so much. If anyone were to have to give me bad heath news, then it would have to come from him. I truly love him like a family member.

Again, men, you are not in this alone. It is not all about you. Your partner suffers just as we do, so never leave them out of the solution.

The results of that year's physical were excellent. No serious issues with me thank goodness.

Before I left the office that day, Sarah came back into the examining room after I had gotten dressed to leave. She gave me a hug and was glad that I did not overreact and decide to go find another doctor. She also handed me a bag of samples with a little of each of the three.

I felt that this gesture was to make up for all that I had gone through because she had forgotten to leave my samples before.

I gave her a big hug, and almost had tears to think that I could have ever entertained the thought of leaving her.

I got my usual prescriptions for the year. I had noticed that Dr. Price, Jr upped the dosage on the main ED pill to 100mg instead of 50mg.

My thinking was just as when I increased to 50mg.

When I did have to fill an order, at least it will be for the maximum dosage allowed. The pill did not come with any higher dosage than that.

In addition, when I cut in half, I still will have 50 mg, which is what I needed then.

I almost forgot to mention the ED medication warning on the television commercials, and in print. That warning is that any man that experiences an erection for more than four hours without returning to normal state to go to the emergency room.

My thought was when a man got to an emergency room with a semi-permanent erection, what the course of treatment would be.

It is my desire that I will never have to find out.

In 2005, I was pissed off about something stupid as usual. I decided to punish myself so I cancelled my annual physical. I told Janice that she could go herself.

Janice is her usual calm manner simply said, "If you want to punish yourself fine. You aint hurting me. Just make sure your life insurance is paid up to date."

When she returned from seeing Dr. Price, Jr, she told me that all went well. She said he was highly disappointed that I did not follow my routine for the past 15 years by cancelling my appointment.

I had even had the crust to ask Janice to ask him for some samples for me. Here I was punishing myself, yet not stupid enough to let an opportunity for some freebies to get past me.

Therefore, when Janice came home and told me that the good doctor had told her that since my physical was cancelled, he would punish me further. She said he refused to give her any samples. If I wanted any, then I would have to schedule my physical.

At first, I thought that Janice was joking. I even asked her is she was serious and really came home empty handed. She just looked at me and told me that she did not stutter and what part of no samples did I not understand.

That got my attention, and I do not mean down below my belly button.

Damn, now I done blew my freebies for at least another year unless I scheduled a new appointment.

Later on that evening of Janice giving me the bad news, I was in my home office with what Janice calls my girlfriend – the computer.

She came in, tossed a small familiar looking pharmaceutical plastic bag on the desk and said, "Here. Dr. Price, Jr said to tell you that if you ever cancel a physical again, you will be cut off for good."

I opened the bag of goodies, and he came through as usual.

He had even given Janice two little gag gifts that were supplied by the pharmaceutical reps that would leave their product samples.

One gift was a keychain that had a small compartment attached. When opened it was designed in the shape of the pill. It held two at a time. In addition, when you pressed the little blue button, it had a little flashlight.

The second gift from a different product line was a pen. When you pressed the top, it opened up and stood erect.

I laughed my ass off.

Leave it to my doctor to have not added any more frustrations that he no doubt knew that I was experiencing.

He knew that part of my cancelling my appointment had to do with my ED situation. Whatever situations were occurring during that time in my life usually was a result of being angry over my ED.

He knew me well enough to know he would not be helping matters any by playing tit for tat. He knew that he would give me a tongue-lashing the next visit anyway so he still had the upper hand.

How cool is my doctor?

Ironically, I had my usual summer cold, cough, and breathing issues just two weeks after the date of my missed physical. When he asked had I eaten that morning, I told him no. I hardly ate in the mornings anyway.

He said, "Good. I will give you a mini annual physical while here to make up for the cancelled appointment."

So a little urine here, blood there, the finger up the ass, and of course the feeling of the balls, and I was out the door in an hour.

To him, the overly cautious doctor that he is would rather know if I had anything seriously wrong then rather than waiting another 12 months.

What an awesome guy.

This Is Not The Worse Medical Condition

Okay men. Get ready for another stupid, male, pride thing that only we can relate to.

One day soon before I check out of here for good, I will get to the point in my life where I can just accept a simple problem solution. I would love to be able to do this without magnifying it to an extreme beyond measure.

I have had my car breakdown on many occasions. I would call Janice upset, and ranting and raving like a lunatic. She would say, "At least you were close to home, and not out in the middle of nowhere."

I had lost jobs over the years also. I would tell Janice how my employer screwed me over. She would simply respond, "Look at the situation as a blessing in disguise. Now you just need to get up off your ass and find something that you really will enjoy."

When I was diagnosed, I was so pissed when I told her what Dr. Price, Jr had recommended. Janice calmly said, "Aint like you were diagnosed with cancer, and had six months to live."

I can continue with endless examples as to how a good partner can keep us grounded if we let them. When our stupidity regards to our pride make us look like asses, we need that special someone to keep things in perspective.

I reached the conclusion that my penis needed and perhaps deserved a little extra dosage to keep him on the right track. When I did come to terms with that, rather than being thankful that there was a higher dosage, I got a case of the ass.

Janice's response to the idea of using 50mg now versus 25mg was, "Many times people have to modify their dosages as time goes on so what is the big deal?"

She then used examples of her daily Thyroid pill. Every so often, her dosage had to be modified. She emphasized what would be the purpose of taking a medication if it did not bring you positive results.

Hmm. She had a point.

Bravo, and kudos once again to my understanding spouse.

Now let us examine the ridiculous rationale that I used to have when it came to spending money on my ED prescriptions.

On the one hand, I have written on how important intimacy in relationships is. However, the next words written are how cheap I am.

On the one hand, I have written on how fortunate that I am to have an understanding spouse. A spouse that has been nothing less than compassionate from day one, on this ED adventure.

Then I contradict myself by saying just how foolish I had acted by being my own worst enemy. There was a solution, yet and still I tried to ignore my problem as if it were not there.

At the time of this writing, I am a healthy 59-year-old. No signs of any form of cancers, heart disease, mental illness (of course Janice would beg to differ on that one), and never been hospitalized. My hypertension and asthma are both under control.

So theoretically, I am a fortunate man.

If ED is all that I have to bitch about, then that should make me a happy camper.

Wrong.

A part of me still feels that I should not be the one with having to deal with being a mechanical man when it comes to intimacy.

I look back now, and try to justify not wanting to spend $80 for six pills, which after cutting in half were actually twelve. When I reflect on being too cheap for something that would improve our love life, I am ashamed of myself.

The same holds true for expecting a return on that investment and getting pissed off when Janice was not in the mood. I used the word wasted, for taking a pill to get ready only to not have a mutual response.

In a loving relationship, the word wasted should never be used in any part of the journey together. Each facet of your sharing is never wasted.

It is of my opinion that too much respect is lost by selling this whole ED condition for more than it is worth.

In other words, men do not, I repeat do not let it ruin your relationship.

Gee, when you begin to look like your spouse after 36 years together, then that speaks volumes for your commitment to be as one.

Now that is not a bad thing to live with. However, men when you treat the other half of you in a disrespectful manner, then that is not a good thing at all.

Those of us ED suffers, and we know who we are, will have a tendency to take out our frustrations on the one that we love the most.

Even if you are not married, still at least that other person in your relationship deserves to be treated respectfully. While you are dealing with your difficulties, your partner no doubt, is dealing with theirs as well as yours at the same time.

I have learned just how much Janice truly loves me by being the wife of an ED sufferer. She has the patience of Job.

Prior to my ED problem in my late 40's, Janice's putting up with me should have earned her the Nobel Peace Prize. The category would have been, "A person who had not killed her husband before driving her to the insane asylum."

Because men are so temperamental, and egotistical, it is my strong belief that of all medical conditions, ED takes the most out of us.

Other conditions can be emotionally, and socially acceptable even though those conditions could be the death of you. However, as long as the penis is not affected, we men do not mind sharing most medical situations.

I know that I should not make the following statement. However, it is my testimony, and my thoughts, so I will go ahead and speak from my heart.

Men would much rather share with their friends that they have contracted a STD, than to admit to having ED. The thinking is that at least with a condition such as STD, it shows that the man is at least having sex.

That is so much better to be up front about, than letting your best friend or family member know that your dick cannot get hard.

For men that are fifty and older, or as they call us, the Baby Boomer Generation, back there in the sixties, STD was a right of passage.

Sounds demented, but in the eyes of others, it was as though you were bragging about how much sex that you were having. More importantly, just how many different females were giving you some.

In addition, a quick trip to the local doctor in the neighborhood, who more than likely knew you, would just give you a shot of penicillin and you were good to go.

Of course, the STD type that I am referring to was not to the magnitude of getting HIV and eventually AIDS.

At least ED will not be the death of you physically, only mentally if you allow it.

I often take long hard looks at photos of my loving wife.

Unless your lover can turn a smile on and off like clockwork, more often than not when you photograph, the feelings captured are for real.

A happy face is a happy face.

A pissed off unhappy face is a pissed off unhappy face.

The cliché, "A picture is worth a thousand words," rings so true to form.

My gift of reflecting back on my photographic memory is not taken lightly. Many people including Janice always admired me for being able to have such a good memory.

So this view master if you will, confirms that Janice and I have had so many more times when we were happy than when we were not.

It has always been, and always will be my commitment to my wife, to try to be a better man each year that we are together. I may not always succeed year to year. However, I can never be at fault for at least trying.

It was my personal opinion that I still had the rights to getting a little pissed off from time to time.

It was also, my opinion that the less angry that I became, the more progress that I was making to overcome that behavior.

If it sounds as though my personal opinions often suck, have no justification, and totally ridiculous, then you are correct.

This just goes to show how the mind can conjure up what thoughts that it wants to. Whether you buy into those thoughts, good or bad, is up to you.

I am certain that ED sufferers will face their worst fears going into their later adult life. At what point and time if those fears become reality, it will be on a personal basis.

For me, my biggest fears are in this order of priority:

The method of my dying is number one.

When the ED pills no longer work, what will I do next is number two.

Guys, there will no doubt come a time when the dosage may have to be increased, which is cool.

All that means to us is that we cannot stretch out our inventory as far. Not a big deal. The fact that we may have to get refills of our prescriptions more often can be justified by just building the cost into the household budget.

If more funds need to be set aside for insuring a satisfying life of intimacy, then you just have to sacrifice another expense. In reality, what would a man not want to sacrifice financially for a happy sex life? I cannot think of anything.

I must not be the only male that would cut the pills in half. The process was like financial planning to me. Of course, even with thinking cheap, I was still ahead of most men since I was always getting free samples throughout the years.

When that time came for me that I discovered that the dosage was no longer doing the job, I went into a state of panic.

People should understand that life will always be changing, thus our own bodies change each year that we live and breathe.

Look at photos, and see how much you change.

Your hair may become grayer, or you have less of it than you had the year before.

Your skin changes, and you may have more wrinkles or bags under your eyeballs.

Other people can visualize these outward physical changes.

However, what about the inward changes that we feel, yet others cannot see?

That is when you must come to the crossroads of acceptance or rejection of your physiological changes. In truth, you cannot do anything about them anyway, so might as well learn to live with those changes.

No one knows our bodies as we do, not even a doctor. Therefore, when we sense and feel that we are going through internal changes, it is the real deal.

Acceptance And Move On

So what do you do when you realize that your penis needs more help this year than the year before?

Accept it to be real, increase your dosage, and move on with your life.

I would still try to continue to take my half a tab, just to push the envelope. I had wanted to see if the old penis still had it in him to rise to the occasion without kicking it up a notch with an entire pill.

Do not kid yourself men.

Your body does not lie to you.

It is not worth the disappointment when you cannot be at your best, and you resort back to feeling like shit. Eventually you will take the second half of the pill if you want to try to salvage the moment, so what difference does it make.

The difference is that old stubborn male ego raising its ugly head one more time.

Disappointing your devoted partner is not fair. Remember it aint just about you.

Let me stop for a moment and clarify the issue on the dosage before I continue.

The pharmaceutical companies understand that no two men are the same. Thus, each company that manufactures pills for ED provides at least three dosages.

That is not only true for ED medications, but most medications have multiple dosages for just about every ailment.

Unless your situation prevents you from getting an erection, all of the time, anytime, then you are safe. Not being able to get an erection at all is matter of a more serious nature.

You will always begin any medication with the smallest dosage until the occasion calls for an increase. I knew why my phobia about the ED meds was to such a degree of alarm.

Remember not being able to have sex even with assistance from a pill was second on my list of biggest fears going into my twilight years.

I went through that psychological crap, and it was not much fun.

Going to my doctor or my dentist is never high on my list of things that I can say that I enjoy doing. I go because I have to, not because I want to.

Having to take a pill to manage my ED, may not be high on my list of things to do either. However, I do because I want to. In order to continue to enjoy a satisfying, active, sex life, then the choice is not up for debate.

As with any medical condition that I have to take a pill for, I understand that the outcome is beneficial.

My blood pressure pills keep me from stroking out, developing kidney failure or heart disease. Would I not be the biggest fool by not taking one lousy little pill a day?

With my asthma, would I not set myself up for being hospitalized or even dying from an attack if I did not carry my inhaler everywhere that I went?

I respond to the only two medical conditions that require medications, with a sense of urgency.

Men, accept having to take a pill to assist you in your love life please. Do not allow your masculine pride to prevent you from having a stress free sex life. It is not worth it.

Pride vs. stubborn pride is two different attitudes.

Pride is a good thing.

Pride works well with one wanting to do their best, and be the best at whatever they are doing.

Stubborn pride is not a good thing.

Stubborn pride prevents you from being open minded, thus becoming very selfish.

Being puffed up with stubborn pride will only lead you to lonely nights, frustrated mornings, ruined vacations, and jeopardizing your relationship.

As an ED sufferer, it was time for me to get over myself. I needed to think more of Janice for the sake of our relationship.

That was the best choice that I had ever made, other than my recovery.

I have not regretted it once.

When I set out to write this book, I had made a commitment to myself to keep things as real as I possibly could. I also wanted to base this on my personal experiences, and not gather data, surveys, and solicit testimonies from others.

I felt that my honest experiences would then allow others to relate to their own personal situations.

My heart's desire is to help to release some of the bent up frustrations that men experience, and create an outlet to vent.

So now is the moment to come to grips with the other reality of living with ED.

That sad reality is that I am certain that many men, as with me, have had some disturbing thoughts along the way.

Having negative and harmful thoughts during, and after those times when our ED raised its ugly head when we had wished that it had not, seems normal.

In sharing those thoughts, although may be painful, and embarrassing, I cannot help but to feel that it is necessary.

I would be less than honest if I did not say that living with ED is an emotional, devastating medical condition. I do not want to excuse the truth as to what I have experienced.

This is from an article that I had read on the internet. I added this to show that this condition is a real, serious, and sensitive subject to talk about.

Definition

By Mayo Clinic staff

Erectile dysfunction (ED) is the inability of a man to maintain a firm erection long enough to have sex. Although erectile dysfunction is more common in older men, this common problem can occur at any age. Having trouble maintaining an erection from time to time isn't necessarily a cause for concern. But if the problem is ongoing, it can cause stress and relationship problems and affect self-esteem.

Formerly called impotence, erectile dysfunction was once a taboo subject. It was considered a psychological issue or a natural consequence of growing older. These attitudes have changed in recent years. It's now known that erectile dysfunction is more often caused by physical problems than by psychological ones, and that many men have normal erections into their 80s.

Although it can be embarrassing to talk with your doctor about sexual issues, seeking help for erectile dysfunction can be worth the effort. Erectile dysfunction treatments ranging from medications to surgery can help restore sexual function for most men. Sometimes erectile dysfunction is caused by an underlying condition such as heart disease. So it's important to take erectile trouble seriously because it can be a sign of a more serious health problem.

Jan. 18, 2008

Living With Ed Can Be Depressing

As promised, now I would like to share some of the pain, and the extreme measures that I have experienced.

Aside from justifying in a humorous format on how to live with ED, there were times when I had felt that death would have been the easiest answer to my frustrations.

The older that I had become, the scarier it had gotten for me. Just the thought of not being able to rely on any form of assistance to live with ED was the ultimate.

I mean just imagine your body becoming immune to any medications that you count on in your daily life to sustain a medical issue that you have.

I live with hypertension. I take medication every day. Imagine that one day your medications no longer work to control your high blood pressure.

I could not even imagine becoming immune to my asthma inhaler, and during an attack where I cannot breathe, that it does not work.

Who from time to time does not live with the condition of being depressed? I mean depression is another book in itself.

Some just have it mildly.

Some have it only when life situations cause an imbalance.

Then there are those that suffer everyday with just getting out of bed, and functioning.

Imagine your medications for depression not working when you need them the most. What would a solution be and if there were an alternative, you would jump right on it.

I see no difference for ED suffers to imagine that one day the wonder pills will no longer work for us.

Now worse than that nightmarish thought, how about feeling that one day the pharmaceutical companies that make these pills decide that this is as good as it will get.

My biggest fear when all of the notoriety of ED came to the forefront of our social consciousness, that some political idiot would find a reason to prevent a cure.

My other fear was that there would be a recall on the pills for having adverse medical side effects.

In my own sick demented brain, my thoughts were, "I don't really give a shit if it kills me dead. If it works I am taking it."

This thinking was like the punch line to a funny story about a man who was a real stud in his hometown. He was buried with no top on the casket, as they could not close it because of his huge erection.

If I were the only male that thought that way, I would care to disagree. Many men may not have admitted that they would cast fear to the wind in lieu of getting a firm erection.

To my surprise though, a political figure, a major league baseball star, and more commercial time prevented any negative press.

With more positive media coverage, there was no intervention by the powers to be to prohibit the production of the medications.

Thank God for that.

Countless times, I have looked up and cursed God for my ED.

Countless times, I have wanted to look my spouse in the eye and ask why she would want to stay with me with my ED.

Countless times, I have had those dark and alone moments when it was just my negative thoughts and me.

Countless times, I have had serious thoughts of no longer wanting to go on living. Those thoughts of suicide were just that – thoughts. There would be no way in hell that I could do such a cowardly deed to my loved ones, and most of all me.

Therefore, what does a man do when he is sitting on the side of the bed, feeling dejected after another frustrating scenario with a loved one. The worst part of the frustration is that you often wonder if you want this to be the last time that it will happen.

You begin to think that if you just went ahead and took every ED pill that you had in your inventory, then if you did not wake up, what a solution that would be.

Just as quickly as thoughts of that scenario came into mind, I dismissed it. With my luck, I would live, and end up in the ER being the laughing stock of the all night staff.

With my top gurney sheet that covered me pitched like a tepee from my erection, I would sound like an asshole explaining how I purposely overdosed on ED medications.

When you have both parties that love each other through thick and thin, better and for worse, it makes you feel more like shit.

You begin to feel as though you let your partner down.

That she deserves better.

That she may be better off without you.

That she may look at you like less of a man.

Living your lives without those awesome "quickies" suck.

That she does not feel that she turns you on.

How do you in the heat of passion just learn to turn off the switch when the light of hope to perform sexually goes dim? Then it gets dimmer, dimmer, and then bingo, the light just goes off all together.

For a man, I do not feel that anything could make us feel any worse. Not even a job loss or financial loss.

Now these thoughts may sound extreme. However, men, when you reach that crossroad in your life with ED, get ready. You will experience thoughts like these and then some.

Once I had felt that I was at my lowest tolerance level of trying to deal with this problem. I had felt that no solutions were working, and that my life sucked big time.

That was until I saw a rat sitting in a corner eating a red onion, and crying like a natural baby. Poor thing. Then I knew times were hard, and my shit was not that bad.

Of course, I am just joking about the rat story.

However, the point is that you can always turn around and see a person so less fortunate. When you do, you will be glad to take your problems less seriously.

I have not completely learned to refrain from expressing my anger in front of Janice. However, it has gotten so much better.

Will the expressions of anger ever go away?

Only time will tell.

Therefore, now that all of the sugarcoated methods of dealing with this dysfunction are out of the way, let us talk alternatives.

I will now share just how this affects my mental ability to be romantic with Janice.

My anger, frustration, and all of the "why me questions" keep haunting me regardless of how much I talk about my situation.

The truth is that you will always feel like less than a man. That feeling is just simply a result of human nature.

People may tell you that your penis is not directly tied to how you should feel as a man. However, stop and think about that for a moment.

That is just like telling a woman with a uterus, vagina, ovaries, and all of the parts that she was given to bare children that she should not feel badly about not being able to conceive.

To think that a woman deep down inside does not feel like she is less than a woman would be naïve.

Although society tends to skirt issues of human sexuality when it comes to realities, the fact remains that sex is a part of our character.

We were all born with these body components to function in life as man and woman. When these components are not clicking on all cylinders, then it is bullshit to believe that it does not affect us to some degree.

I am a recovering drug addict, and I was always told that once an addict, then always an addict. I had heard that theory so often that I always felt as though there would never be a time in my life where I could kick my habit.

Words are so powerful that you can accept them into your own reality without realizing the affect.

If I had bought into the belief that what I heard was truth, then I would not be where I am today – drug free for 38 years.

So In Conclusion

Accepting our living with ED as men is just something that we have to do. Period.

We may not have to like it.

We may not understand it.

We must have open and honest communication with our partners.

We must be able to talk open and honestly with other men about this medical problem.

We may still be pissed off and frustrated.

We may still have all of the above feelings and more.

However, at the end of the day, your ass still has a problem getting an erection.

Therefore, when you are all alone with your inner true feelings, you always end up feeling like shit. You will always question where for art thou the direction your manhood is heading.

The issue is not all of the above.

The issue is you either shit or get off the pot.

As they say down in the South, you either fish or cut bait all day.

The sooner that we learn to live with these feelings, yet move on to getting some medical help, is the issue.

The bigger picture is you can be happier living with the solution than being unhappy by not accepting the solutions.

Whatcha gonna do fellas?

Your balls are in your court.

Therefore, my desire and purpose of writing this book was to help to open up honest dialogue for men and their partners. Let us not forget the open dialogue with our physicians and other male friends without being ashamed.

I had mentioned the "no longer being here" statement to illustrate to the degree this depressed feeling can take a man.

However, in my opinion thinking about suicide is normal for many people at some point and time in their lives. The idea may simply be a fleeting thought based on a real time situation to that person.

What matters the most is the idea is that person's idea based on their viewpoint and problem solving abilities.

If the person's situation is small or large, it matters not.

To the person dealing with any situation, what matters to them is their outlook on their circumstances and not anyone else's.

I listened, and still listen to people who are cancer survivors and wonder where they got the strength and courage to face their disease. Most are in your face type of people who refused to allow their cancer to not rule their lives.

I have tried my best to put myself in their shoes and ask, "Bruce, how would you deal with being diagnosed with cancer?"

There is no answer as I have not faced that dilemma, and hope that I never will.

Each of us can place ourselves in a hypothetical situation and diagram an easy answer to a difficult question. Nevertheless, truth be told, we do not know how we would handle anything until placed in that situation for real.

Therefore, I cannot be any more honest when I say that living with ED is very difficult. Any man that says differently is not being honest.

Please understand that I am learning to live with this condition, yet still hating everything about it emotionally and physically.

I hate the frustrated nights.

I hate the being angry with God.

I hate not being at a point where I feel comfortable with a female pharmacist.

I hate going to work in the morning angry after a frustrating night.

I hate going each year for my physical and all is well except having ED.

I hate joking with others about this problem, yet deep down feel embarrassed.

Lastly I hate looking my spouse in the eyes and saying I am sorry.

Yes, I understand that hate is a strong word to describe a human emotion. However, that is the only word that I can use to best describe my true feelings.

There is nothing that may ever change how much I hate the condition. The fact of the matter is that I took action, and learned to manage it better.

Just as I was about to finish my writing, I was informed that one result from my August 2008 physical indicated that my PSA reading was elevated.

Great! Just what I needed to hear. Now I will have ED and cancer. At that rate, I may never have an erection again.

Dr. Price, Jr advised me to go have a prostate biopsy. He is not an alarmist like some doctors. However, he is proactive. That and the fact that he had told me that his father and brother were both diagnosed with prostate cancer, he did not want to have me take a risk.

That sounded good enough for me. He even referred me to their doctor, Dr. Brooks. I figured since both his dad and brother were doctors also, that I would be in the best capable hands.

Although I understood that the prostate gland could play a major role in causing ED, the word biopsy scared the shit out of me.

To know that another person is inserting some object up your ass is not a pleasant thing to look forward to, yet necessary.

When Dr. Brooks explained the procedure in full detail, I tried not to squirm too much in my chair. I love taking photos of family, nature and the ocean while on vacation.

However, the idea that someone was going to stick a camera up there and photograph my prostate was a different story.

He told me not to worry. He had done hundreds. Sure easy for him to say.

I ran into my neighbor, Brother Harry, the morning of the biopsy while walking our dog Shultzi. Brother Harry was a good man, good neighbor and deeply religious, unlike me.

He told me that he had the procedure, and was thankful as he was diagnosed with cancer and had treatment. Gee just what I needed to hear.

I asked did it hurt. Of course, he said it was uncomfortable, but no, it was not painful.

I slapped him high five, and then drove over to Janice's job so she could take me to the office for the biopsy.

Once prepped, and lying there on the table with my butt to the sky, he had nerve to ask if I had wanted to watch on the monitor.

I said thanks, but I would pass. Cartoons or CNN would have been fine, but the thought of viewing something going in my behind and probing my prostate was not my cup of tea.

I must admit that Dr. Brooks was nice and explained every detail of the procedure. He even went as far as telling me what I would be feeling.

That gave me some comfort level. I would at least know if I felt something, or heard something, I would not freak out.

What the son of a bitch did not tell me before he began was that he was going to snip not one or two, but twelve tissue samples.

I did not find out until he got past the first two and I asked were we done, and he said no there were ten more to go.

Ten more?

Dear God, this will take foreverary.

Guess he figured why not be honest with me now. What was I going to do, get up from the table and leave?

Therefore, I just laid there and took it up the ass like a man.

The machine that is used sounds like a cap gun. Each time he took a snip, it made a snapping sound so loud it worked your last nerves.

Having a female in the room to store the tissue samples while you were lying with your hairy ass exposed was also embarrassing. I guess to her, it was just another man's ass, and after awhile we must all look alike. You see one you see them all.

Once finished I loved the question, "Now was that so bad?"

Here I was feeling like kicking his ass, and he is grinning and saying how things went smoothly.

Now I love buying and sending a dozen roses to Janice but for no other reason than to express my deep love for her.

I also love buying jelly doughnuts by the dozen.

I love the phrase, "cheaper by the dozen."

I just did not enjoy the Urologist taking a dozen tissue samples of my poor little prostate gland.

When I saw Harry later that afternoon, I told him all went well and really did not hurt as he had said.

However, when I asked why he did not tell me how many samples they were going to take, he smiled and said, "Because you would not have went!"

Nice guy.

I waited the four days including the weekend for my results.

When the doctor left a voice message on my cell with the good news that all twelve samples were negative, not any signs of cancer, I cried.

I then screamed aloud in the car.

Next, I called Janice.

Growing old aint for sissies, and true as one's body begins to come apart at the seams it is a bitch.

As Uncle Bobby says, "The wheels are starting to come off the wagon."

Yes, if men live long enough, then eventually there will be some medical issue that will no doubt affect your ability to get an erection.

How you handle that situation when it arises is up to you.

I am going to close now.

There is so much more to write about.

However, sharing my personal experiences is not like getting into the statistics on this topic. It is my desire that men will follow up and do their own research on the subject.

Gathering statistics, sharing them, and accepting them does not make a person feel any better. It is only my opinions that gut level human emotion does more for expressing how one feels than sharing statistics.

When a person has a real, life-changing crisis that is not the time to be spewing off statistics. I feel that what matters the most in times like those is having someone who has walked in your shoes that can share, and lighten the load.

So for more information regarding erectile dysfunction, please utilize all of the available online tools that you can. Gather as much information as you need. Be careful though to not gather more than you need. Too much is worse than not enough.

I will again emphasize that online information, and reading materials are fine.

I will also emphasize again that nothing takes the place of establishing that good, solid relationship with your physician and your partner.

I guarantee that you will feel so much better about your health conditions once you build those foundations. Remember that ED is a health condition. You did not do anything to bring it on yourself.

I trust that either way you choose to look at dealing with ED, the best choices that I have outlined will make living with ED easier – not harder!